THE LAYMAN'S BIBLE COMMENTARY

THE LAYMAN'S BIBLE COMMENTARY
IN TWENTY-FIVE VOLUMES

THE LAYMAN'S
BIBLE COMMENTARY

Balmer H. Kelly, *Editor*

Donald G. Miller   *Associate Editors*   Arnold B. Rhodes

Dwight M. Chalmers, *Editor, John Knox Press*

VOLUME 24

THE LETTER TO THE
HEBREWS

THE LETTER OF
JAMES

THE FIRST AND SECOND LETTERS OF
PETER

John Wick Bowman

JOHN KNOX PRESS
Atlanta

10 9 8 7 6 5 4 3

Complete set: ISBN: 0-8042-3086-2
This volume: 0-8042-3084-6
Library of Congress Card Number: 59-10454
First paperback edition 1982
Printed in the United States of America
John Knox Press
Atlanta, Georgia 30365

PREFACE

The LAYMAN'S BIBLE COMMENTARY is based on the conviction that the Bible has the Word of good news for the whole world. The Bible is not the property of a special group. It is not even the property and concern of the Church alone. It is given to the Church for its own life but also to bring God's offer of life to all mankind—wherever there are ears to hear and hearts to respond.

It is this point of view which binds the separate parts of the LAYMAN'S BIBLE COMMENTARY into a unity. There are many volumes and many writers, coming from varied backgrounds, as is the case with the Bible itself. But also as with the Bible there is a unity of purpose and of faith. The purpose is to clarify the situations and language of the Bible that it may be more and more fully understood. The faith is that in the Bible there is essentially one Word, one message of salvation, one gospel.

The LAYMAN'S BIBLE COMMENTARY is designed to be a concise, non-technical guide for the layman in personal study of his own Bible. Therefore, no biblical text is printed along with the comment upon it. This commentary will have done its work precisely to the degree in which it moves its readers to take up the Bible for themselves.

The writers have used the Revised Standard Version of the Bible as their basic text. Occasionally they have differed from this translation. Where this is the case they have given their reasons. In the main, no attempt has been made either to justify the wording of the Revised Standard Version or to compare it with other translations.

The objective in this commentary is to provide the most helpful explanation of fundamental matters in simple, up-to-date terms. Exhaustive treatment of subjects has not been undertaken.

In our age knowledge of the Bible is perilously low. At the same time there are signs that many people are longing for help in getting such knowledge. Knowledge of and about the Bible is, of course, not enough. The grace of God and the work of the Holy Spirit are essential to the renewal of life through the Scriptures. It is in the happy confidence that the great hunger for the Word is a sign of God's grace already operating within men, and that the Spirit works most wonderfully where the Word is familiarly known, that this commentary has been written and published.

THE EDITORS AND
THE PUBLISHERS

THE LETTER TO THE
HEBREWS

INTRODUCTION

Authorship

The Letter to the Hebrews was early known and employed
throughout the extent of the Church, East and West. It was first
quoted in Rome by Clement, one of the Church Fathers (A.D. 95).
Thereafter it was employed in the West by several writers of the
second and third centuries. The church of Alexandria appears to
have been the first to consider that Hebrews was written by Paul
or reflected his thought. It was suggested that it had been written
by Paul in Hebrew and translated into Greek by Luke. Others in
the third century held that the style was non-Pauline though the
ideas were considered to be Paul's. One of the Church Fathers of
this century, Origen, held that "God only knows certainly" who
wrote the epistle. An early papyrus manuscript of the third century, recently discovered, which emanates from Egypt and possibly Alexandria, places Hebrews immediately after Romans and
before First Corinthians, thereby indicating the belief that the
epistle was from the pen of Paul.

From the period of the Reformation to modern times there has
been great diversity of opinion on the matter of authorship. Cal-
vin held it to be from Paul's pen, while Luther thought of Apollos
as the author and Erasmus suggested Clement of Rome. Others
gave their vote to Barnabas. One startling suggestion was that the
letter was written by Priscilla. More recent writers continue to
propose a variety of authors, no one of whom has won a majority
of supporters.

Readers

There is as much disparity of opinion regarding the Christian group addressed in the letter as in the matter of authorship.
From the early fourth century there have been those who have be-

lieved that the letter was addressed to the church in Jerusalem, or
at any rate to the Palestinian church. Others have thought of a
Jewish-Christian community in one of the large centers of the
ancient world, such as Alexandria, Rome, or Ephesus. Some suggest a Hellenistic-Jewish group within the Roman church. ("Hellenistic" refers to the influence of Greek ideas and culture upon
the Jewish religion.) Others hold that the letter was addressed to
Christians as such, either including both Gentiles and Jews or
composed exclusively of Gentiles. In this last case, of course, the
title of the epistle would be a misnomer.

Date

Two sets of facts have generally been emphasized as determin-
ing the date to be assigned to the writing of the letter. The first
of these has to do, on the one hand, with the apparent use which
the author of Hebrews has made of some of the Pauline epistles
and, on the other, with the fact that Clement of Rome (A.D. 95)
quotes from Hebrews in his letter to the Corinthian church. Thus
Deuteronomy 32:35-36 is used by Paul in Romans 12:19 and by
Hebrews at 10:30. Similarly, in both Romans 4:17-21 and Hebrews 11:11-12 and 19 reference is made to the age of Abraham
and Sarah at the time of the promise of the birth of Isaac.
Clement refers to Jesus as "the high priest of our offerings, the
defender and helper of our weakness" (see Heb. 2:18; 3:1; 4:15).
He also describes Jesus as one "who, being the brightness of his
majesty is by so much greater than angels as he hath inherited a
more excellent name" (see Heb. 1:3-4). These two considerations
suggest a date for the letter somewhere between A.D. 56 and 95.

The second consideration suggestive of a date is to be found
in the fact that the readers had already suffered one persecution
for their faith and were now facing the likelihood of a second
(10:32-34; 12:3-11). There has been, however, little unanimity
among interpreters as to which persecutions are meant. The following have been suggested as possibilities—the one under Claud-
ius in A.D. 49 (Acts 18:2); the well-known persecution under
Nero in A.D. 64; the destruction of the Jewish state in A.D. 70;
and the persecution under Domitian in A.D. 95.

Suggested dates for the writing of the epistle are as follows:
between 58 and 95, 85-110, 75-80, 70-95, about 95, 65 or 66,
and sometime in the middle 60's.

A New Solution

From the above statement of the history of the problem, it will be apparent that there can be no authoritative pronouncement relative to the circumstances, author, readers, and date of writing of the Letter to the Hebrews. The best minds of the Church have given their attention to the solution of these problems and have found themselves unable to reach a united conclusion with regard to them. The Christian student, accordingly, if he is to face the problem at all, must do so with an open mind and a sincere endeavor to make the best of the data available.

During the past decade certain significant facts have come to our attention which would appear to suggest the possibility of a new solution. These data are principally of two kinds—*first*, the rediscovery of or re-emphasis upon the fact that the Judaism of the first Christian century was by no means a single phenomenon; and *second*, the discovery of the Dead Sea Scrolls at Khirbet Qumran and the valleys south of Wadi Qumran which have materially increased our knowledge of one type of contemporary Judaism in the first Christian century. It will be well at this point to state the position which, in the light of these recent developments, will be supported in this commentary. This is to the effect that (1) the author and readers of the Letter to the Hebrews belonged to a single group in the Palestinian situation to be designated as "Hellenistic-Jewish Christians"; (2) this group lived together at some undesignated point, possibly at Sychar in the Roman province of Judea (which included both the old Judea and old Samaria); (3) the occasion of writing was the author's earnest desire to stimulate greater zeal for the distinctive elements in the Christian gospel among Christians who, because of their "liberal" background, were intrigued with that gospel's similarities to the best in Judaism; and (4) the epistle was written shortly before the destruction of the Jewish state in A.D. 70, when the Qumran sect was forced to abandon the center of its influence at Khirbet Qumran. It is our intention to suggest that both the author of the letter and his readers were converts from the ranks of Hellenistic Judaism, and that the readers had fallen under the influence of the teachings of the Qumran sect—an influence which had not intrigued the author, though he found it convenient in view of his readers' known interest to state the message of the gospel in terms made familiar by the teachings emanating from Khirbet Qumran. The author, though he belonged to a section of the Christian community whose background was quite other than the Hebraic Judaism out of which Paul sprang, was nonetheless familiar with Paul's writings and generally sympathetic with his doctrinal position, while at the same time his statement of the fundamental teachings of the Christian faith followed a pattern different from that of Paul. The letter then may be dated in A.D. 65 or 66, at the beginning of the First Jewish War and almost synchronous with the date of Paul's death in Rome.

The Hellenistic-Jewish Christianity of First-Century Palestine

First-century Judaism was by no means a unified faith. There were sectarian cleavages within it, some of them characterized by bitter hatred toward other branches of Jewry. The major cleavage is generally designated by the terms "Hebraic Judaism" and "Hellenistic Judaism" (see Acts 6:1). Paul himself employs this terminology and claims to have belonged to the Hebraic side (Phil. 3:5; II Cor. 11:22). The terms employed to designate the two branches of Judaism have a reference which is far wider than the respective languages spoken by the two parties, though the use of different languages is not excluded. "Hebraic" and "Hellenistic" refer rather to the total cultural patterns adopted: on the one hand, adherence to strict Jewish patterns of life, and on the other, accommodation to Greek cultural patterns. Nor does the factor of place necessarily have any bearing upon the problem. Paul was a native of Tarsus in Cilicia and therefore a resident of the Hellenistic world outside of Palestine, and yet he was a typical example of the Hebraic Jew. Contrariwise, the Sadducees, whose center and entire life involvement was the Temple in Jerusalem, were notable for having adopted the Hellenistic culture pattern.

To one like Paul who had been converted from the strictest element (the Pharisaic) within Hebraic Judaism, it became clear that culture patterns have no significance for the Christian faith. Such was the nature of his argument with Peter at Syrian Antioch, which he reports in Galatians 2:11-21. We read, however, in Acts 6 and 7 of a sharp controversy which developed between the Hebraic-Jewish Christians and their Hellenistic-Jewish Christian brethren.

We have little enough to go on here—merely the account of the controversy itself as narrated in the sixth chapter and a statement of the beliefs of the Hellenistic-Jewish Christians as contained in Stephen's speech in chapter 7. It seems clear, however, that the Hellenistic party were generally committed to what one might term the more "prophetic" point of view. This included the idea proclaimed by the prophets as early as Amos in the eighth century before Christ that the true faith had universal significance and so was equally for all peoples. The same striking idea is abundantly illustrated in Stephen's address—that God's revelation of himself to men is independent of land (Acts 7:2, 9, 30-31, 36, 38). This revelation is also independent of cultural background, as Moses' culture was largely that of the Pharaohs (vss. 17-22) and of Midian (vss. 23-29). It is likewise independent of a particular house of worship, both that which Stephen calls "the tent of witness in the wilderness" and Solomon's Temple (vss. 44-50). And finally, the implication is that God's revelation is independent even of the people of the Law (the Jews), for Stephen makes it clear that it was characteristic of Israel that they rejected the revelation which God gave through selected individuals called "prophets" (vss. 25-26, 35-36, 51-53).

The Hellenistic-Jewish Christian faith as proclaimed by Stephen is reflected throughout Hebrews, notably in 2:5-18, where the author argues on the basis of Psalm 8:4-6 that Jesus in his incarnation has come "that by the grace of God he might taste death for every one" (vs. 9). The same point is made in connection with our author's choice of Melchizedek, "king of Salem, priest of the Most High God" (7:1-3), as one who though he was in no sense a Jew yet was a blessing both to Abraham and to all his descendants, including the Levitical priesthood (7:4-10).

The unworthiness of "rebellious" Israel is also portrayed with telling effect (3:7-19), in contrast with faithful prophetic spirits like Abraham and his descendants, Joseph and Moses, "the prophets," and others of their type who suffered persecution at the hands of the forefathers of the Jews themselves (ch. 11). The true faith's independence of land and even of the Holy City of Jerusalem is brought out with telling force by Hebrews (11:10, 14-16, 23-31; 13:12-14).

Finally, Stephen's thesis that the true faith does not depend upon the use of a particular house of worship is directly related to the major theme of Hebrews. This letter, like Stephen, takes its start from the instruction which God gave Moses in Exodus

25:40. Moses was to erect a house of worship "according to the pattern which was shown" him on the mountain (Heb. 8:5; Acts 7:44). The writer maintains that the true house in which God's worship is to be carried on is a spiritual or eternal one (9:11-12). That is, it is a house made up of living personalities (3:6)—a thought also worked out by Paul (Eph. 4:11-16; Col. 2:19). In addition to these major similarities between the message of Stephen and that of Hebrews, there are minute ones of a striking sort of which but one may be mentioned here, namely, the mediation by angels of the Old Testament revelation (Acts 7:53; Heb. 2:2).

It seems clear from the above comparison that the author and his readers, who as we have said belonged to a single group of second-generation Christians (Heb. 2:3-4), must have been Hellenistic-Jewish Christians of the type represented by the "seven" of Acts 6:5-6. This element in the Early Church, dating back to at least A.D. 35, was scattered after the persecution that arose as the result of Stephen's martyrdom "throughout the region of Judea and Samaria" (Acts 8:1). If we allow some thirty years to intervene before the writing of Hebrews, it will perhaps appear not unlikely that they should have drawn together at some central point. And what better place could be imagined than a spot near the ancient capital city of Samaria, possibly at Sychar?

This possibility moves into the realm of probability when the incident recounted in John 4 is recalled (see especially vss. 5 and 39). For, as has been shown recently, the interests manifested by the Gospel of John are those of the Hellenistic-Jewish branch of the Christian Church, and it is striking that the city of Samaria should be spoken of as a center of evangelism both in John 4 and in the Book of Acts (8:4-25) in connection with the evangelistic work of Philip, who along with Stephen was a member of the Hellenistic-Jewish Christian community. At Mount Gerizim near Samaria the ancient Samaritans had erected a temple in competition with that at Jerusalem (John 4:20). It is, therefore, the more striking that Jesus should declare to the woman of Sychar that "the hour is coming when neither on this mountain nor in Jerusalem will you worship the Father" (John 4:21), and that "the true worshipers will worship the Father in spirit and truth" (vs. 23); while the author of Hebrews in like vein argues that "the sanctuary and the true tent" in which Christian worship is to be maintained is one "not made with hands, that is, not of this creation" (Heb. 8:2; 9:11). Similarly, "Mount Zion," "the city of the living God" which Christians are said by our author to approach for worship, is "the heavenly Jerusalem" (Heb. 12:22), for as he says, "Here we have no lasting city, but we seek the city which is to come" (13:14).

The Discovery of the Dead Sea Scrolls

The above distinction between Hebraic- and Hellenistic-Jewish Christianity affords us only one-half of the picture suggestive of the setting in which the Letter to the Hebrews had its origin. The momentous discovery of the Dead Sea Scrolls beginning in 1947 has provided us with the other half. Though it is true that the "monastic" community at Khirbet Qumran was the center of the sect, yet the scrolls are witnesses to the fact that cells or "camps" were maintained throughout all Palestine, a fact to which Josephus apparently is referring when he speaks of the Essenes as those who "have no certain city but many of them dwell in every city."

It should be evident, then, that there was every chance of the Hellenistic-Jewish Christian community in Palestine coming into contact with and being influenced by this sect. Numerous similarities may be pointed out between the teachings of the Qumran group and those of the Letter to the Hebrews. For example, the group spoke of themselves as the people of the (new) "covenant." There can be no doubt that the reference of this term is to Jeremiah 31:31-34, the passage quoted in Hebrews 8:8-12. And the coincidence of thought between the Qumran Scrolls and Hebrews is seen to be the more striking when one notes that of the twenty-eight references in the New Testament to the "new covenant," exactly one-half are to be found in Hebrews alone. Reference has already been made to the fact that in Hebrews 8:2 coupled with 3:6 the teaching emerges that the Christian community is the true "house" or "temple" of God. This same claim is made for itself by the Qumran community. Both the Qumran sect and Hellenistic-Jewish Christians speak of themselves as "the enlightened ones." Both claim to be a people who possess "truth" in a peculiar way. Both groups claim to have experienced the "power" of God in a special way. Both claim to constitute a "fellowship of the saints" including those on earth and those in heaven. Both consider themselves to be tested and proved by God.

But while there are similarities of the type indicated between the teachings of the Qumran sect and Hellenistic-Jewish Christianity—similarities which are more or less parallel with other groups within Judaism and Christianity, due to the fact that all draw upon the common source of the Old Testament Scriptures —the dissimilarities in teaching between the two groups are even more striking. This is particularly true of their concepts of high priesthood and sacrifice. In fact, it is exactly at this point that the teachings of the Qumran community and of Hellenistic-Jewish Christianity as exemplified by the Letter to the Hebrews are found to be in violent opposition to each other. This phenomenon more than any other points to the conclusion that the Letter to the Hebrews was written in the context of and contemporary with the existence of the Qumran community at Khirbet Qumran.

It is, for example, known that this sect looked forward to the appearance of a messiah who would be of the House of Aaron and might therefore be termed a "priestly" or high-priestly messiah. The author of Hebrews, however, shows that "our Lord was descended from Judah, and in connection with that tribe Moses said nothing about priests" (7:14); he concludes in consequence that Jesus' high priesthood depends, not upon his earthly connections, but upon the fact that he is of the Melchizedekian order, that is, that he is an eternal figure (6:20; 7:11-22). It would seem from these and like references in Hebrews that the author is concerned to deny outright the Qumran claim that the Messiah was to be of the tribe of Levi. His point is exactly that Jesus Christ, *because of his eternal character as Son of God* (1:1-4), combines within his own person both kingly and high-priestly messiahships. This is in flat contradiction of the point of view elaborated in the Qumran community, and it would seem, therefore, that the letter is written in the context of the teaching of that community.

There is a significant difference as well in the matter of the character of the sacrifice to be offered in the worship of God. It is true that the Qumran sect did not ban the use of animal sacrifices. They did, however, proclaim a day about to dawn within Israel when "atonement will be made for the earth more effectively than by any flesh of burnt offerings or fat of sacrifices." This is teaching derived quite clearly from passages like Hosea 6:6 and Micah 6:6-8. Nothing in the scrolls, however, suggests the type of sacrifice to be offered by Jesus Christ as the High

Priest of his people who "entered once for all into the Holy Place, taking not the blood of goats and calves but his own blood, thus securing an eternal redemption" (9:12). Nor is there any suggestion anywhere in the scrolls akin to the further statement of our author that "the blood of Christ" (the Messianic High Priest), "who through the eternal Spirit offered himself without blemish to God," will "purify your conscience from dead works to serve the living God" (9:14). The Old Testament precursor of such a Messianic High Priest is, of course, the Suffering Servant of the Lord, and of such a figure offering such sacrifice the Qumran Scrolls know nothing.

It has often been remarked that the only Old Testament sacrifices which were a matter of concern to the author of Hebrews were those performed by the high priest on the Day of Atonement. On no other day of the Jewish religious year was the high priest constrained by law to sacrifice at all. But for that day all sacrifice must be offered by him alone. In consequence, for the author of Hebrews only the sacrifices offered on that day were remotely comparable to that of the eternal High Priest Jesus Christ; and by the same token, for him the Christian life constituted one continuous Day of Atonement, even as for the Apostle Paul it was one continuous Passover (see Heb. 10:19-31; 12:22-24; 13:12-16; and I Cor. 5:6-8). It seems deeply significant, therefore, that in the Qumran Scrolls no reference to the Day of Atonement should thus far have been found. It is as though Hebrews were pointing to the significant lack at this point in the teachings of the Qumran community, and calling Hellenistic-Jewish Christian readers' attention to the uniqueness of the Christian faith in having a Messianic High Priest of an eternal rather than an earthly order, whose sacrifice of himself has given to the Christian life the character of an everlasting Day of Atonement.

As has been said already, two references in the epistle itself are perhaps indicative of a date. The first is at 5:12, where it is stated that the readers "by this time . . . ought to be teachers." It would seem that the community had been together for a considerable length of time after the scattering abroad indicated in Acts 8:1. The other reference is that pertaining to the two persecutions—one already passed (10:32-34), the other on the horizon (12:3-13). If we may assume that the first of these persecutions was that which arose about Stephen in approximately A.D. 35, the second may be conveniently reckoned as associated

with the First Jewish War in A.D. 66-70. During this period, as we
now know, the Qumran community was thriving, and its influence
throughout the Roman province of Judea was widespread. We
may well conclude, therefore, that the occasion prompting the
writing of Hebrews was the attractive nature of this sect's teachings for Christians who had emerged from the Hellenistic-Jewish
community and for whom accordingly, "temple," "land," "sacrifice," and "holy city" were of as little concern as for the Qumran community. In the meantime, too, we know that the center
of Christian evangelistic effort had passed from Jerusalem to
Syrian Antioch, bypassing Samaria and its Hellenistic-Jewish
community on the way! That community had never become a
band of "teachers" or evangelists with a gospel of God's redemptive activity on behalf of all men everywhere and with a zeal for
carrying that gospel to the ends of the earth, though the creative
effect of the persecution out of which the community had sprung
surely gave early promise of such zeal and Christian statesman-
ship (Acts 8:1, 25; Heb. 5:12; 10:32-39). All signs indicate that
the early fires had burned low in this Christian group. They were
becoming "fainthearted" (Heb. 12:3), and they fretted under the
discipline imposed by Christian living (12:4-11). Like the church
at Laodicea, they were now "neither cold nor hot" (Rev. 3:15)—
a dangerous attitude exposing such "fainthearted" Christians to
the attractions of the nearest second-best religious interest. So far
as Judaism was concerned, that second-best was to be found in the
high motivation and zeal, as well as in the exalted claim to be the
"elect" community (the genuine Israel of God), on the part of
the Qumran sect. It was here the attraction lay, then, for this
Hellenistic-Jewish Christian community at Sychar. And we know
that coupled with this attractiveness to be found in the highest
element of the old faith, the fires of nationalism were burning
high in the early 60's in the Holy Land—fires which burst into
the flames of open revolt against Rome in A.D. 66. But neither
nationalism nor a second-best religion is good enough for followers of Jesus Christ, who himself "suffered outside the gate" of
the Holy City (Heb. 13:12). Accordingly, his followers must "go
forth to him outside the camp" of Judaism, "bearing abuse for
him" (13:13).

The Message

Hebrews has been termed "the Epistle of the Covenant" and "the Epistle of the High Priesthood of Jesus Christ." Both of these characterizations represent the truth in some measure. Neither singly nor together, however, do they give us a comprehensive picture of the message of Hebrews. Each represents a major stress of the letter, and each clearly gives evidence of the contemporary situation with which the author and his readers are concerned. But both elements may be said rather to constitute "means" which our author employs in presenting his message and endeavoring to arrive at the goal he has in view, rather than the goal itself.

The over-all theme of the letter, and therefore the message which its author is endeavoring to present, may be phrased thus: *the responsibilities and privileges of "sonship"*: (1) of the "Son of God" as eternal High Priest; (2) of the "sons of men" as members of God's household. As will appear from scanning the outline of the letter, there is a constantly recurring interplay of emphases upon the nature and work of the unique Son, on the one hand, and of similar factors relating to the "sons" on the other. Jesus Christ is first and last the unique Son of God (1:1-4). As such he is in his own person and work separated from all prophets, angelic intermediaries (1:5-14), and even such a great leader of God's people as Moses himself (3:1-6). He is uniquely over God's house rather than simply a member of it, in virtue of his being God's Son (3:6).

But Jesus Christ has chosen through the Incarnation to identify himself with the "sons of men" or more specifically with that particular group among men who may be called sons of Abraham, that is, true members of the household of God (2:9, 16). He has thus identified himself with man with a view to man's salvation and has gone through the most trying and debasing of man's experiences—experiences brought on by man's sin and resulting in his spiritual and moral death (2:14-18). In searching for a religious analogy to which he might compare this work of the eternal Son of God, the author hit upon the unique plan of presenting Jesus' work in terms of high priesthood and the sacrifices performed by the high priest on the Day of Atonement. However, unwilling to expose his argument to the attack of any who might point out that Jesus did not belong to the Levitical priesthood and therefore that the analogy of the high-priestly work was inadequate in his case, he came forward with the creative suggestion that Jesus' high priesthood is similar to that of Melchizedek—an eternal one performed in an eternal tabernacle and associating itself with eternal sacrifices (5:8-10; 7:15-28). The argument is a valid one because of the intrinsic nature of the being of the Son of God, a type of being transcending all earthly existence (1:1-14).

The second part of the author's thesis is as important for his goal as the first. It rests upon the underlying assumption that although sons of men are in their essential being far beneath the "Son of God," yet there is a certain kinship involved which does not exist between the latter and any other of God's creatures—not even angels. This unique kinship makes possible not alone the Son's identification with the sons of men in their low estate and sufferings (2:10-13), but also their identification with him in his responsibilities and privileges. For as Christ was "faithful over God's house as a son" (3:6), so they are called to constitute "his house" (3:6); and as he was called to be the high-priestly Mediator "on behalf of men in relation to God" (5:1-10), so the demand is laid upon them to be "teachers . . . [of] the word of righteousness" (5:11—6:8). Moreover, as the responsibility laid upon the Son of God included his high-priestly work, in which he sacrificed himself that men might draw nigh to God through him (7:1—10:18), even so it is incumbent upon the "sons" as lesser priests, who now have access to the "sanctuary" in God's eternal tabernacle, to "draw near with a true heart in full assurance of faith, with . . . hearts sprinkled clean from an evil conscience and . . . bodies washed with pure water" (10:19-31). And as Jesus, "the pioneer and perfecter of our faith," endured to the end of the earthly race set before him (12:1-2), so the sons are called to endure, to accept without protest the discipline required for Christian growth (12:3-11), to remain faithful in their allegiance to the revelation of the Christian message (12: 18-24), to recognize the divine lordship over their lives (12: 25-29), and to accept every obligation which that sovereignty of God imposes upon his true worshipers in the realms of both religion and social ethics (12:28—13:17).

Finally, the author sees that just as Jesus was called upon to suffer "outside the gate" of the Holy City (13:12), so it is incumbent upon the sons that they also "go forth to him outside the camp," that is, outside the contemporary Judaism in which the author's Hellenistic-Jewish readers were raised, so "bearing abuse for him" while they "seek the city which is to come" (13:12-16). In view of all that has been said above, there can be little doubt that the Letter to the Hebrews was a clarion call to Hellenistic-Jewish Christians to sever the bonds which bound them with Judaism, and that at the opening of the First Jewish War it proved to be one of the effective means toward making complete and irrevocable the final break between the Christian faith and the older Judaism. Both faiths accepted the Old Testament as Scripture, but the incarnate life and work of Jesus Christ gave to the Christian Church a standard lacking in Judaism, by reference to which that Scripture must henceforth be judged and interpreted.

OUTLINE

The Redemptive Power and Lordship of God's Son. Hebrews 1:1—2:18

Manifesto Regarding the Son of God (1:1-4)
Proof of the Manifesto from Scripture (1:5-14)
Redemptive Implications for the Sons of Men (2:1-18)

The Gospel Call to Become God's House. Hebrews 3:1—4:16

The Son's Faithfulness Over God's House (3:1-6a)
The Thrice-Repeated Gospel Call (3:6b—4:16)

The Nature of the Son's High Priesthood. Hebrews 5:1—7:28

Qualifications of a High Priest (5:1-10)
Qualifications of Mature Sons (5:11—6:20)
The Son's Melchizedekian High Priesthood (7:1-28)

The Efficacy of the Son's High-Priestly Work. Hebrews 8:1—10:18

Summary Statement (8:1-6)
Ineffectiveness of the Old Covenant (8:7—9:10)
Effectiveness of the New Covenant (9:11-28)
The Once-for-All Aspect of the Son's High-Priestly Work (10:1-18)

The Response Required of Sons to the High-Priestly Work of the Son. Hebrews 10:19—13:17

Summary Statement (10:19-31)
Examples of Faith (Hope) (10:32—11:40)
Exhortation to Endurance as Sons (12:1-29)
The Communal Life of God's People Outside the Gate (13:1-17)

Epistolary Conclusion. Hebrews 13:18-25

COMMENTARY

THE REDEMPTIVE POWER AND LORDSHIP OF GOD'S SON

Hebrews 1:1—2:18

Manifesto Regarding the Son of God (1:1-4)

Hebrews begins not as a letter but as an essay or address. There is no salutation or indication of any kind relating to the identity of the readers (see Introduction). Two points stand out in these first four verses: (1) the author's desire to indicate genuine continuity between the revelations given during the old and new periods, and (2) the superior character of the revealing medium in the new period.

The God who reveals himself and his will "of old" is the same God who speaks to us in his Son. The men and women chosen as the vehicle of the old revelation are called "prophets." A prophet is by definition one who has a message from God and a commission to declare it to his generation. The older revelation was piecemeal, fragmentary, lacking in unity. It was given, too, in "various ways"—in dreams and visions, through a burning bush, by the "angel of the covenant," in a "still small voice," and in other ways.

In direct line with this prophetic revelation, and yet in noteworthy contrast to it, God has now spoken to his people through "a Son." As God's medium of revelation to man this Son is in direct line with the prophets; in his essential nature or being, however, he is quite different from them. This Son is described in two ways: first, as to his essential being, and second, as to his functions. Fundamentally he is Son of God and so bears the stamp of the "glory of God"—a phrase which in both Hebrew and Greek stands for the showing forth of God's real nature. This Son is, so to speak, as closely related to the Father as are the rays which stream forth from a source of light to the light itself, as sunbeams to their central sun. Moreover, he is the "very stamp" or impressed seal bearing the name of God in his human nature— the signature of God, so to speak, impressed as in wax on the universe.

And because the Son is these things in himself, he has functions
which are far above those of all other beings. He is the agent of
creation and so is at the beginning of history; he is also the "heir"
and so is at its end (vs. 2). And as he is at the beginning and at
the end of history, so also he is in its middle, providentially "up-
holding the universe." But this Son has a relation not only to the
whole of God's created universe, but more particularly to man.
In this connection Hebrews conceives of him as man's Sin-
purifier and Lord (vs. 3). This twofold function is one upon
which the author will dwell at great length throughout the letter.
In saying that the Son has "sat down at the right hand of the
Majesty on high," the author quotes from Psalm 110:1, a Psalm
which takes us to the heart of the message of Hebrews (see 5:6;
6:20; 7:11).

These opening verses introduce us to a unique conception of sonship which is to carry through the epistle and throw light upon
much of its teaching. The Son of God is an eternal figure. But the
author is interested in what he does in both time and eternity,
and he begins with the Son's function in time. Christians are
already living "in these last days" (vs. 2), that is, in the period
in which the Son serves as the Mediator of God's word to man.
The exact phrase occurs only here. But a like phrase appears in
9:26; I Corinthians 10:11; and I Peter 1:20; 4:7. Other passages,
too, such as I John 2:18, mean that the end-time has come. The
Christian Church, therefore, is already living in the end-time, and
Christ is God's final and definitive revelation of himself to man.
He has already made a cleansing for man's sins and has sat down
in eternity "at the right hand of the Majesty on high." The name
"Son" is accordingly the greatest to be "obtained" by any being
—greater than "angels," a word which in both the Hebrew and the
Greek simply means "messengers" and which may be applied to
every vehicle of God's revelation to man (vs. 4).

Proof of the Manifesto from Scripture (1:5-14)

The author of Hebrews is concerned to show that the name of
"Son" places Jesus Christ "above every name that is named, not
only in this age but also in that which is to come" (Eph. 1:21).
In making this demonstration he calls upon a series of texts from
the Old Testament in the Greek translation (the Septuagint). The
first of these, in verse 5, is from Psalm 2:7. The first part of the

quotation was used by the voice which addressed Jesus at his baptism (Mark 1:11). But neither here nor in 5:5 does the author show any knowledge of this baptismal experience of Jesus. However, he does conceive of the Psalm as giving us the Father's voice speaking to his eternal Son. Psalm 2 is a Messianic or "royal" Psalm in which the reigning king or contemporary "anointed one" (messiah) prefigures the coming great One who, in a final sense, will fulfill the role of Messiah. It is in the same way that the author understands the second quotation (from II Sam. 7:14). Actually the words were originally spoken by the prophet Nathan to David in the name of the Lord. There can be no doubt that the author knows this, but as before he conceives of Jesus Christ as fulfilling the promise in a far richer and deeper sense than originally intended. The same is to be said of the third quotation (from the Greek version of Deut. 32:43). All three quotations are words of God concerning his eternal Son, either at the beginning of his ministry or even at the Incarnation (note in verse 6: "when he brings the first-born into the world").

By way of contrast with the above description of the eternal Son's exalted function as God's Messiah in the world, the author now calls upon Psalm 104:4 to illustrate the transitory nature of the angelic host. In the Hebrew the psalmist had spoken of God as One "who makest the winds thy messengers, fire and flame thy ministers." Every created thing, then, may serve as a minister of God's purpose. The Greek translation, which is followed in Hebrews, reversed the order of the words to read as they are quoted in verse 7. This change suited the purpose of the author admirably, for it lays emphasis upon the transitory nature of all of God's created messengers. Angels, together with all of his servants, are transient by nature, as are winds and flames of fire. All depend upon God for their existence at every moment.

Hebrews employs another royal Psalm (Ps. 45:6-7) in verses 8-9. In the Psalm the reigning "messiah" or "anointed one" is addressed in language that stresses the exalted function of God's emissary as he rules among men. The righteous or saving nature of the king's function as "messiah" is stressed, a function corresponding to the view of Christ which appears throughout the epistle.

With a yet bolder stroke the author now calls into service Psalm 102:25-27 (vss. 10-12). These verses were originally intended by the psalmist to refer to the Lord as the Creator of the universe. Hebrews unhesitatingly applies them to Christ, the eternal Son. This is in accord with the author's previous remark that the Son was the medium through whom God had made the world (vs. 2). Once again it is his purpose to show the eternal character of this Son. Finally (vs. 13), to conclude his description of the exalted nature of the Son he again quotes Psalm 110:1, as at verse 3 above. And again, by contrast, all others of God's messengers are described as "ministering spirits sent forth to serve, for the sake of those who are to obtain salvation" (vs. 14).

It is clear from this chapter that the author knows only two categories of existence—God (with whom and in whom he includes his eternal Son), and creatures (all created beings, "angels," prophets, mankind generally, and all of nature). One senses the fact that there was a type of teaching to which the Christian readers of this essay had been subjected and whose tendency was to dispute the clear-cut nature of this division, or at any rate the inclusion of the Messiah with God as his eternal Son (see Introduction).

Redemptive Implications for the Sons of Men (2:1-18)

Responsibility for Response on Man's Part (2:1-4)

This short section comprises the first of a number of "hortatory sections" to be found in the letter (see 4:11-16; 5:11—6:8; 10:19-39). These passages indicate plainly that the author feared that his readers were in danger of drifting away from the tradition which they had received as Christians. It is clear that the community to which this essay was sent belonged to the second, or possibly the third, generation of Christians. They were not among "those who heard" the Lord but were numbered among those who had received the tradition from that earliest group. However, the essay cannot have been written very late in the first Christian century, for it is evident that this community had not received the gospel in written form. They had merely "heard" it (vs. 1), and it had been "attested" to them (vs. 3). They were a link in the chain of tradition which went back to the Lord Jesus, and they were an early link in that chain (see further 5:11-14).

At this point (vs. 2) the author introduces another traditional belief with regard to angels. This is to the effect that the Old Testament revelation, and particularly that at Mount Sinai in the giving of the Law, had been made through the instrumentality of angels. The Greek translation of Deuteronomy 33:2b (a passage in which the Hebrew is obscure) reads "his angels were with him at his right hand." A part of Judaism interpreted this to mean that the Law had been given at Sinai by angels as mediators, and the same idea appears at two places in the New Testament (Acts 7:53; Gal. 3:19).

This idea of the Old Testament revelation as given at the hands of angels, however, did not work against its validity. The Law was accepted as "valid," and its commands as the word of God and therefore to be kept (vs. 2). The author's argument is from the less to the greater. If a revelation transmitted by angels is to be respected, how much more that delivered through the Son. The new revelation has come to the Christian community from the Lord (the Son) himself, through the first generation of the Apostles and those who, like them, heard him speak; and God himself had applied the message to the hearts of believers, granting his Holy Spirit to seal it to the Church (vss. 3-4).

"Signs . . . wonders . . . miracles"—these are the technical words employed by the Early Church to describe the wonderful works of Jesus and those of the Holy Spirit (see Matt. 14:2; Acts 2:22). The word translated "gifts" actually means "distributions" or "divisions" (see 4:12). The idea, however, is probably like that in I Corinthians 12:4 and 11—the Spirit is one and his gifts many.

The Son's Death and Exaltation (2:5-9)

In this section the author begins to come to grips with the major problem with which he wishes to deal, namely, the redemptive activity of the Son of God on behalf of the sons of men. We have already seen that the angels were but "ministering spirits" (1:14) on behalf of these sons. It is not, therefore, with the angels for their own sake that God is concerned (vs. 5), but rather with the redemption of the sons of men and more particularly with "the descendants of Abraham" (2:16). Accordingly the author indicates the present condition of these sons, their future high destiny, and the manner in which this destiny is to be accomplished.

He first states unequivocally the high destiny which God has appointed to man. He does this in terms of Psalm 8:4-6. In the Hebrew the Psalm indicates that man is made "little less than God." As, however, the Greek translation reads "a little less than the angels," the quotation here served the author's purpose of contrasting the angels with men. In verse 6 "man" and "son of man" are in Semitic parallelism, both terms meaning simply "man." Both authors—of Psalms and Hebrews—no doubt had in mind the original saying in Genesis 1:26 to the effect that God has appointed man his viceroy over all his creation. God has placed "everything in subjection under his feet." For the author of Hebrews the dividing line between the two ages, history and eternity, is the Incarnation. Christians are already living "in these last days," the age of the "Son," not in the age "of old," the age of the prophets (1:1-2). Accordingly, "the world to come, of which we are speaking" (vs. 5)—that is to say, the eternal age—has already arrived for Christians. They have already tasted of the "powers of the age to come" (6:5). The signs and wonders and gifts of the Holy Spirit referred to in verse 4 are without doubt a part of these powers. It is clear, then, both from the testimony of Scripture and from Christian experience that God has subjected all things in both ages (the historical and the eternal) to man. It is equally clear that however high and exalted the station of angels may be conceived, the "glory and honor" attendant upon such power as God has committed to man as his viceroy is something which they do not experience.

Nevertheless, "we do not yet see everything in subjection" to man (vs. 8). Man has not yet fully come into his heritage. However, there is one man who has already attained the highest estate which God has appointed to man generally. This man is Jesus, the Son. Jesus accepted man's low estate, a condition described by the psalmist as being "lower than the angels" (vs. 7). He did this "that by the the the grace of God he might taste death for every one" —that is, thoroughly to identify himself with man even in the extremity of "death" (vs. 9). Because Jesus accepted this humble estate of man he was "crowned with glory and honor." Identification with man in death involves identification with him in the high estate which God intended for him. This, it should be noted, is exactly the logic followed by Paul in Philippians 2:5-11. But the logic of redemption works also in reverse. As Jesus is identified with man, so man is identified with him. The experiences of each become the experiences of the other; by the grace of God, Jesus Christ tastes of death on behalf of everyone, and so everyone experiences salvation through him.

Identification of the Son with the Sons (2:10-13)

The author now argues for the necessity of the Son's humiliation if he would become the Savior of men. His basic assumption is that an essential unity between Savior and saved is necessary in order that the end in view may be accomplished. The best expression of the principle is found in verse 18: "Because he himself has suffered and been tempted, he is able to help those who are tempted." The justification for this principle of a unifying experience as necessary for Redeemer and redeemed no doubt lies in the prophetic ideas of "corporate personality" and of the corporate nature of experience. In neither Old nor New Testament does the individual stand alone. Rather he is conceived at all times as being a part of a larger group—the nation in the Old Testament, the Christian fellowship in the New Testament. If the individual is to be saved, therefore, he will be saved as a member of the group, and similarly the Savior is one who arises out of the group and is one with it in experience.

It is in the light of this principle that the author declares it "fitting" that God, the Creator, "for whom and by whom all things exist," should mature Jesus as man's Savior by a process of suffering. Salvation here is spoken of as man's being brought "to glory" (vs. 10). The word is used because of its appearance in the Psalm quoted in verse 7. "Glory and honor" represent the exalted position of viceroyalty which God has purposed for man. It is a condition in which man as the "image" of God (Gen. 1:26) reflects the latter's power and personality as his appointed viceroy. Jesus as the Mediator of this experience to man is called "the pioneer of their salvation." Sometimes the Greek word employed here is translated "captain" or "leader." In any case, the picture is of one who, as a member of the fellowship, moves ahead, leading the way to ever higher ground of experience. This progressive experience is termed by the author a maturing one ("perfect"; see also 5:9, 14; 6:1; 7:28; 9:9). The language suggests the maturing of the individual person to adulthood and implies successive stages of growth. It is a matter of common experience that without "suffering" such maturing is not possible in the world as we know it.

Paul places stress upon man's justification in the sight of God; Hebrews lays more emphasis upon man's consecration or sanctification. This is no doubt because the Savior's function which the author wishes to stress is that of "High Priest," and such terms as "sanctification," "holiness," and "consecration" are those which normally applied to the work of the high priest. Both the sanctifying High Priest and the people whom he prepares for the worship of God are said to "have all one origin"; that is to say, they have a community of experience in their common humanity (vs. 11).

In proof of this essential unity between Savior and saved, the author calls upon three passages of Scripture in which the principle is presented. The first of these is Psalm 22:22, a so-called "Servant" Psalm. This is a Psalm in which is pictured the "Suffering Servant of the Lord" in much the same fashion as that redeeming figure is described in Second Isaiah. The Psalm is one of the most frequently quoted in the New Testament, first in Matthew 27 and Mark 15 in describing the agony of the Cross, and thereafter by the various New Testament writers in appropriate contexts. Hebrews therefore is following in the usual tradition of the Early Church in identifying Jesus with the "Suffering Servant" who saves by vicariously assuming the suffering and death common to all mankind. The second and third quotations, in verse 13, are from Isaiah 8:17-18. There the prophet and his followers are declared to be the "signs and portents" of the working of God in Israel, a prefiguring of God's saving activity on behalf of man through Jesus and the fellowship which clusters about him in the Christian Church.

The Sons' Condition of Slavery (2:14-16)

The author now repeats what he had already said in verse 11 to the effect that Savior and saved "have all one origin," or as he now phrases it, "share in flesh and blood." He now adds, however, the ultimate purpose of this identification with mankind—namely, the destruction of "the devil" and the deliverance of man from "fear of death." Death is generally conceived in Scripture as man's last great enemy (Gen. 2:17; I Cor. 15:26; Rev. 20:14). The opposite of death is life or salvation, and this is always conceived of as the gift of God and under his power. Naturally, therefore, death belongs to the kingdom of Satan or the Devil, and it represents his final power over man. The nearest scriptural parallel to the series of ideas with which our author is working at this point (flesh and blood, death, the Devil, lifelong bondage) is to be found in Paul's treatment of the kindred theme in various passages in Romans (5:12-21; 6:1-11; 7:1-5; 8:1-39).

There now follows a repetition of much the same thought as we have already seen in verse 5 above—"it is not with angels that he is concerned but with the descendants of Abraham" (vs. 16). Between the two verses, however, there has been a marked advance in thought, and in consequence the mode of expression exhibits two striking differences. First, in verse 5 and following, as we have seen, it was of man in general that the author spoke, and the contrast was a general one between angels and mankind. Here, on the other hand, the contrast is between angels and "the descendants of Abraham." Second, in verse 16 the thought is expressed in the language of Isaiah 41:8-9, in which the descendants of Abraham are identified with the Servant of the Lord.

Consequence for the Son (2:17-18)

The author finally draws the conclusion (which he has already mentioned in vss. 10 and 14 above) of the necessity of identification on the part of the Savior and his "brethren." This identification is necessary if the end in view is to be accomplished. Now, however, for the first time he states that end in terms of the high-priestly work of Christ, and so begins to sound the greatest note of the letter as a whole. The "merciful" character of this High Priest will find expression in 4:14-16 and 5:1-10. His "faithful" character is the subject of 3:1-6a. It is characteristic of the style of Hebrews to introduce in this way items of interest which will later receive fuller development at the author's hands.

"To make expiation" for sin is not again mentioned in the letter in so many words. However, expiation was the task of the high priest on the Day of Atonement, and that service is elaborated at considerable length in 8:1—10:18. "Expiation" is essentially the removal of stumbling blocks between persons, in this case the stumbling block of sin between God and man. The principle of identification between Jesus as High Priest and man goes only so far as his being "tempted," not sinning. On this point the author is very insistent (see 4:15; 7:26).

THE GOSPEL CALL TO BECOME GOD'S HOUSE

Hebrews 3:1—4:16

The Son's Faithfulness Over God's House (3:1-6a)

Worship of God requires a house of worship. The author therefore now introduces us to the thought that God through Jesus
Christ calls unto himself the people who shall constitute such a
living house of worship. This call is a "heavenly" one; that is to
say, it has a divine origin (vs. 1), "heaven" often appearing in the
contemporary Judaism as a substitute for the name of God himself. The Christian readers who have experienced this call are now
called "holy," that is, consecrated or dedicated to the service of
God.

The author wishes to stress the faithful character of Jesus Christ,
through whom the call comes to man to become God's house. The
latter part of verse 1 might well be translated: "Will you give
your attention to the one sent to be High Priest (as we confess
him to be), that is, to Jesus?" This is the second time that the
historical name "Jesus" has been mentioned by the author (see
2:9), and in both cases it is in connection with the incarnate life
and ministry and designated service which Jesus has performed
on behalf of man. Nowhere else in the New Testament is Jesus
called "apostle." The English word is a slight modification of the
Greek, and both together have behind them a Hebrew term employed only of a special messenger who carries with him the full
authority of the one sending. Jesus, accordingly, as High Priest
comes to us with all the authority of God himself, and the author's
present point is that he has proved "faithful" in his exercise of
this authority (vs. 2).

Moses, too, was one sent upon a special mission by God, and
he was faithful in fulfilling the service appointed to him; but by
comparison with Christ's function that of Moses was a menial
one, as is shown by the word "servant" (vs. 5) employed in Numbers 12:7, which our author is quoting here. The choice of Moses
in this connection for purposes of comparison is the obvious one,
since it was through Moses as leader that God constituted Israel
as his people at the Exodus. On the occasion of the choice of a
new promised land God has chosen Moses' opposite—Jesus

Christ. But here the comparison ends, for whereas Moses was merely a "servant," Jesus Christ is "a son" (vs. 6), through whom as God's Mediator all things are accomplished (see 1:2). Jesus Christ is the Creator, or as is said here, "the builder of a [the] house" (vs. 3). The builder is, of course, God himself (vs. 4), but the author in his thinking has long since brought Christ into union with God as Son (vs. 6; see 1:1-4).

The contrast between the two figures runs throughout this section. Both are pronounced faithful in their several spheres of service, but Moses is to be kept in his place. He was faithful, but as a servant only; Christ is also faithful, but "as a son." Moses was faithful "in God's house"; Christ is faithful "over God's house." This contrast between Moses and Jesus Christ is clearly indicative of the temptation to which the readers of this letter are exposed. It has to do without doubt with the character of the revelation represented on the one hand and the other by Moses and Jesus Christ. As clearly as in the letters of Paul, Moses here stands for Law, Christ for grace. Paul, it is true, was interested primarily in the ethical side of the Law, whereas Hebrews' main interest lies in the ritual side. But this is probably because of the particular nature of the problem presented by the readers of Hebrews, for there can be no doubt that they were being attracted by the claims of the Qumran sect to represent the "people of the covenant" under Moses (see Introduction). For the moment, by way of reply to this the author contents himself with the remark that Moses' highest function was "to testify to the things that were to be spoken later," that is, to those things which characterized the saving activity of Jesus Christ as great High Priest (vs. 5). Moses was, therefore, to be superseded by God's "son."

The Thrice-Repeated Gospel Call (3:6b—4:16)

Urgency of the Call and Steadfastness Required (3:6b-15)

If faithfulness was required of the Son, it is also required of the "sons." This generally is the main theme of the sections which follow in chapters 3 and 4, in which the author in an almost inextricable fashion mixes instruction and exhortation.

He begins with the assurance that Christians are "God's house" provided they fulfill certain conditions. There is a remarkable underlying sense of the unity between the Hebrew people and the Christian Church at this point which must not be overlooked. Both

Moses and Christ had been said above to have been faithful with
reference to "God's house" (vss. 5-6). It is startling, immediately
following that discussion, to read that Christians are this house,
that is, they are the people of God (vs. 6b; see also Eph. 2:19,
22). Underlying this contention is clearly the idea that God has
been for centuries calling out a people for himself. Accordingly,
it should be clear that the "call" is for the people who hear it,
whether Jews or Christians; that the required response to the
call is one of faith or faithfulness; and that the resultant people
responding to this call are one. In the sections which follow, the
unity of the call and of its essential message, or gospel, is to prove
one of its most notable features.

The "hope" (vs. 6b) in which Christians are to find "confidence" and "pride" is of an eschatological nature (6:18-20),
which is to say that essentially it refers to the completion and acceptance of Christ's saving work by God in the eternal order.

The author, as is his custom, bases his entire argument in this
section upon a passage from the Old Testament, Psalm 95:7-11.
This Psalm was one regularly employed in the synagogue in connection with worship on the Sabbath (the Hebrew word meaning
"rest"). This was appropriate in view of the Psalm's stress upon
the subject of "rest" and the possibility of God's people entering
with him into "rest." It serves the author's purpose admirably also
inasmuch as "sabbath" or "rest" was one of the terms employed
by the Jews for "salvation." Moreover, the Psalm with its reference to the wandering in the wilderness under the leadership of
Moses lent itself to a comparison of the two faithfulnesses here
involved—that of the leaders, Moses and Christ, on the one hand,
and that of the people of God on the other.

The original events referred to in the Psalm are those involving
the murmuring of the people of Israel when confronted with lack
of food and proper drinking water in the wilderness (Exod. 15:
23-24; 17:7; Num. 20:2-5). The Psalm also illustrates the note
of urgency that is struck whenever God's voice is heard, in view
of the striking manner in which the quotation begins—"Today."
"But exhort one another every day," says our author, "as long as
it is called 'today'" (vs. 13). The urgency of the call arises in
every case out of two factors—first, God speaks to each generation calling it to himself; second, the response is required on the
day on which it is heard. Moreover, in this and the following sections the responsibility of man for response to the divine call is

emphasized throughout. If men do not respond, it is because they harden their hearts against God's call; it is because they test and try him; it is because they "always go astray in their hearts"; it is because they have not known God's ways (vs. 10). God holds every generation accountable for such failure. The source of such an attitude is "an evil, unbelieving heart," and its end is to "fall away from the living God" (vs. 12).

On the other hand, the promise is held out that we shall "share in Christ," or become partakers or fellows with him, in the privileges which are his as Son over God's house, provided "we hold our first confidence firm to the end" (vs. 14). God demands steadfastness, confidence, assurance, and faithfulness of his people at all times.

Failure of Israel at the First Call (3:16-19)

On at least three occasions the divine "call" has been given to man to become God's people. The first of these is that referred to in the Psalm which has just been quoted. The people involved are the Israelites, and the occasion is the Exodus from Egypt (vs. 16). The author's major concern here is to place the blame for Israel's failure to receive the promised "rest" squarely where it belongs, namely, upon Israel and her sin. He advances from stage to stage in his argument by means of question and answer. His argument may be stated in positive fashion as follows: (1) there need be no question about God's first call having been heard; Scripture makes it clear that those involved both heard and rebelled against the call (vs. 16a); (2) the group concerned included the entire Israelitish people who came up out of Egypt under Moses (vs. 16b); (3) for forty years God was provoked by their clear attitude of rebellion (vs. 17a); (4) their "bodies fell in the wilderness" on account of their sin (vs. 17b); (5) God properly punished their disobedience, swearing that that generation "should never enter his rest" (vs. 18); (6) it is clear, therefore, that the generation concerned were properly punished on account of their "unbelief" (vs. 19).

Openness of the Promise Shown by the Second Call (4:1-10)

The argument now shows that the promised "rest" is still available for the people of God. This conclusion is drawn in 4:9: "So then, there remains a sabbath rest for the people of God." The passage begins as a hortatory section—"let us fear lest any of you be judged to have failed to reach" God's rest (vs. 1). On the whole, however, it is a doctrinal section, and this also appears in verse 1 ("while the promise of entering his rest remains"). There is obviously here the underlying assumption that, when God gives a promise, it is bound to be fulfilled at some time or other. If this does not occur in the lifetime of the immediate generation to which the promise is spoken, then it remains open to be received by some future generation. In this expectation is seen a sense of continuity between the Old and New Covenants like that to which reference has already been made in previous sections (1:1-4; 3:1-6a).

This assumption has ground in the Psalm (Ps. 95) which is employed here. In fact, the author sees in the repetition of the call in the Psalm a clear indication that the promise is still available to the people of God. Fundamentally, to say that the promise remains open until it is fulfilled is to say that God is the "living" God (vs. 12) and that he is "faithful," faithful to fulfill his promises (10:23; 11:11).

The generation to which the author writes represents a third occasion on which the promise is opened to man. There are thus three stages in the presentation of the promise, as follows: first, to the Moses-Joshua generation (3:16; 4:8), second, to the generation of those to whom the Psalm was addressed (3:7; 4:7), and third, to the Christian community (4:2, 9, 11).

In view of the nature of the argument here, a more definitive phrase than "good news" for the contents of the promise is required (vs. 2). Actually, the Greek at this point reads, "for we also have been evangelized even as they." The verb ("evangelized") has a long history behind it in both Hebrew and Greek, and long before the Christian era it had acquired a technical connotation, being applied specifically to the preaching of the message of God's redemptive activity on behalf of man. This meaning of the verb is found in its final Old Testament development in Second Isaiah in such a passage as 52:7. It is easy to see that the "good tidings" there (that "God reigns") becomes in Matthew 4:23 "the gospel of the kingdom" and in Luke 4:18 the "good news to the poor." Then, too, the very nature of the argument in Hebrews that the promise remains open requires that the "good news" announced on each occasion shall be essentially the same. Otherwise the argument has no validity.

It is invalid to object to such reasoning on the ground that the promise formerly given through Moses and Joshua had to do with the acquisition of a land, whereas the promise through Christ refers to eternal salvation. Such a compartmentalizing of human experience is foreign to the thought of Scripture, where there is rather a sense of the oneness of life and experience as a whole. God is interested in and concerned about the salvation of that whole. Accordingly, in the Scriptures, God's promise to save man in any part of his being involves his being saved in every part. The author, therefore, sees no incongruity in conceiving of the promise through Moses and Joshua, through David, and through Jesus Christ as representing essentially the same gospel message of God's redemptive love.

For much the same reason, perhaps we should accept the alternate reading given in the margin for the second half of verse 2, rather than that found in the text: "the message which they heard did not benefit them, because *they were not united in faith with those who heard.*" The passage is as difficult to understand in the Greek as in the English, but the margin seems to have the best evidence in its favor. If adopted, it should be understood to refer to the fact that faith is the required normative response to the gospel promise, and that such faith unites in a great fellowship down the centuries those who receive the salvation offered in the gospel. The next verse would seem to support this view: "For we who have believed" enter into that fellowship and enjoy the common rest because we are "united in faith with those who heard" and accepted it.

Verses 3 and 4 elaborate the idea of God's "rest" by drawing upon the Genesis account of the seven days of creation (Gen. 1). The seventh day of the creation week was the day of rest for God (Gen. 2:2)— God's "sabbath." This period of rest may be thought of also as that salvation into which God calls men to enter with himself (vss. 4-5; see also Ps. 95:11). A word of warning should be sounded perhaps at this point, lest the idea that salvation involves enjoying the rest of God and that man "ceases from his labors as God did from his" (vs. 10) should be so interpreted as to suggest that in the future life Christians will have nothing whatever to do! Such an entire cessation of activity is nowhere taught in Scripture with regard to either God or man. In Jewish thought, "sabbath" stood for serenity, peace, and harmonious enjoyment of the works of creation on the part of both God and man. For the Jew the Sabbath has always been a day of joyful experience of all the good things that God has made. Fasting and mourning on this day are forbidden by rabbinic law. It is a day for luxurious living, for calling in one's friends to enjoy a meal, for dressing up in one's best, and for expressing generally the delights of godly living. There can be no doubt, therefore, that when our author speaks of ceasing from labor, it is this sort of experience that he has in mind, contrasted with the fretting and anxiety attending the usual occupations of six days of the week.

Exhortation to Response at the Third "Call" (4:11-16)

Again exhortation and doctrine are mingled together. The section opens with exhortation: the need for the human response of the "sons" to the divine call is a constant emphasis in this book. We have already observed this at 3:6, 12 and at 4:1; we shall meet with it again (see 6:1-8). Moreover, the "disobedience," or alternatively the "unbelief" (3:19) which caused it, is held up as a warning to those who experience God's third call through Jesus Christ (vs. 11).

The discerning power of the "word of God" is presented as a first stimulus to the response required of sons (vs. 12). Only here and in 13:7 does the phrase "the word of God" appear in this letter. But its equivalent is found in such phrases as "the promise" (4:1), "good news" (4:2), "the message which they heard" (4:2), "the elementary doctrines of Christ" (6:1), and possibly others. This, then, is the gospel message, and our author unites with it a number of participles and adjectives by way of defining its function and power. To begin with he says that it is "living," a favorite expression of his intended to indicate at once the power and the relevance of various aspects of the Christian faith.

The adjectives and participles which follow serve to show how this living word of God functions in relation to those to whom it comes. Because it is living, it is therefore "active," being "sharper than any two-edged sword." We are reminded of the Suffering Servant's description of himself in Isaiah 49:2—"He made my mouth like a sharp sword." In Revelation 1:16 the exalted Christ is also said to have "a sharp two-edged sword" proceeding from his mouth. The expression is a figurative one, indicative no doubt of the saving and condemning or judging aspects of the word, according as it is received or rejected by those who hear. Moreover, the activity of the word takes the form of "piercing to the division of soul and spirit, of joints and marrow," that is, of thoroughly searching out and exposing the innermost secrets of the sons of men, a thought also expressed in the words "discerning the thoughts and intentions of the heart." This discerning function of the word is picturesquely indicated by saying that "all are . . . laid bare" before God, an expression which refers to the twisting of the neck of the victim in sacrifice in order that the knife may be inserted, or to the bending back of the head of an opponent in a wrestling bout (vs. 13).

A second inducement to Christians to respond to the third gospel call which they have heard is to be found in the gracious character of the Son as "high priest" (vss. 14-16). This is the third time the author has used this term with reference to our Lord. In the two previous passages (2:17; 3:1) it was his faithfulness in performing the function assigned to him by God that was stressed. But now a new factor is brought into prominence, that of his rich experience. For he "has passed through the heavens" (vs. 14). This idea no doubt is related to that expressed in 2:9 where we saw him "crowned with glory and honor." But here for the first time there is a suggestion of his return to earth with a view to the saving of his people. The Jewish high priest went into the sanctuary of Tabernacle and Temple and then came out to bless the people at prayer. Jesus Christ as our High Priest does the same; he, too, returns from the sanctuary on high that he may take hold of our hands and lead us "near to the throne of grace" (vs. 16).

The phrase "yet without sinning" (vs. 15) should be strengthened. The Greek reads "without sin," and is to be equated with the parallel passage at 7:26—"separated from sinners, exalted above the heavens." Probably in both these places the reference is to the difference which sin makes in human experience. The author, then, wishes to say that Jesus was tempted in every way that man is, except for those ways in which sin itself determines the nature of the temptation. He had never given in to sin, and consequently he could not even be tempted as those who have once succumbed to sin are tempted.

THE NATURE OF THE SON'S HIGH PRIESTHOOD

Hebrews 5:1—7:28

Qualifications of a High Priest (5:1-10)

Appointment and Humanity (5:1-4)

We have now arrived at the central and most important section of the letter, that which deals with the nature of the Son's high priesthood and with his work. These two subjects will occupy five and a half chapters, or a bit more than two-fifths of the book.

In the present section the author selects for his purpose two qualifications of the high priest—namely, his divine appointment and his humanity. The high priest, he points out, is from the side of man and is to act for man, even as the prophet was from the side of God and was appointed to act as God's spokesman (vs. 1). The high priest thus becomes a true representative of man before God, "since he himself is beset with weakness" such as is experienced by all men. The high priest is human, because he shares the weakness of the men whom he represents before God. He is himself a sinner and "is bound to offer sacrifice for his own sins as well as for those of the people" (vs. 3).

Actually the only day in the entire Jewish year when it was incumbent upon the high priest to offer sacrifices was the Day of Atonement (Lev. 16). On this day the high priest offered a bull "as a sin offering for himself . . . and for his house" (Lev. 16:6). "Some of the blood of the bull" he took and sprinkled on the mercy seat in the Holy of Holies (Lev. 16:14). Only thereafter was he qualified to kill "the goat of the sin offering which is for the people" and to take "its blood within the veil," sprinkling it upon the mercy seat in the Holy of Holies (Lev. 16:15). In the Jewish Mishnah (the law book which gives us a view of the contemporary Jewish customs) one entire book is devoted to the exact manner of the high priest's functioning on the Day of Atonement. And both Old Testament and Mishnah paint for us a striking picture in accord with Hebrews' delineation of the high priest and his work: he is a servant of the people, acting on their behalf, and one with them in standing in need of forgiveness and salvation.

The present passage abounds with references of an accurate nature, showing a good knowledge of Jewish law. For example, the "gifts and sacrifices" of verse 1 are probably the "cereal offering" and "flesh" sacrifices specified under the Law (Lev. 2:1, 4; 7:12, 15-18). Again, it is likely that "the ignorant and wayward" specifies the two classes of sinners recognized under the Law—namely, those who committed offenses against the Law through ignorance (Lev. 4:2; 5:14, 17), and sinners "with a high hand," that is, those who voluntarily disobeyed the Law although it was known to them (Num. 15:30).

The second qualification of the high priest is that of divine appointment (vss. 1, 4). Actually only Aaron among Jewish high priests was personally called by God (Exod. 28:1). Thereafter, the high priest was a member of the tribe of Levi, which was descended lineally from Aaron. But the selection of a particular high priest was confused throughout the history of Judaism following the Exile. Under the Maccabean princes, for example, the high priesthood had been seized as the prerogative of the ruling house. Under the Romans, the high priest was often appointed by the provincial government of Judea. Actually his inauguration was accomplished either by anointing or by investiture.

The Jews generally accepted as high priest one drawn from the tribe of Levi, and therefore they recognized such a one as qualified for the office by the mere fact of birth. The author of Hebrews suggests that the High Priest acknowledged by the Christian Church is one who occupies the office with the same high qualification enjoyed by Aaron at its inception—the call of God alone.

Fulfillment by the Son (5:5-10)

The author now shows that the two qualifications of high priesthood above indicated (humanity and the divine call) are both fulfilled in the case of Jesus Christ. In asserting the divine appointment, the author makes use of two royal Psalms (Pss. 2:7 and 110:4). The first of the quotations ("Thou art my Son, today I have begotten thee") probably is intended to have reference to the voice which spoke from heaven to Jesus at his baptism. However, as reported by Mark (1:11) that voice employed only the first part of the quotation from Psalm 2:7 ("Thou art my . . . Son"), substituting for the second part of the verse a clause from the Greek translation of Isaiah 42:1 ("my beloved, in whom I am well pleased"). For the quotation from Isaiah, which refers to the ordination of the Suffering Servant, Hebrews substitutes Psalm 110:4

("Thou art a priest for ever, after the order of Melchizedek"). It seems certain that Jesus applied Psalm 110 to himself (see Mark 12:36). Possibly, therefore, the author of Hebrews understood Jesus to mean that the eternal Father had used the words of this Psalm in speaking to his eternal Son, applying their significance to him.

The author wishes to say that our Lord was himself aware of appointment from God as high-priestly Messiah. Jesus did not choose these high offices for himself. But equally he was not unaware of his divine appointment. He had good reason, as he was addressed by the heavenly voice, to know himself both Messiah and High Priest of his people.

The second qualification for the high priesthood (humanity) was also met by Jesus Christ. For although, as we have already seen, he was in his essential being Son of God (1:1-4), nonetheless he "learned obedience through what he suffered" (5:8). In this connection Hebrews lays particular stress upon the "prayers and supplications, with loud cries and tears" which Jesus offered "to him who was able to save him from death" (vs. 7). Undoubtedly the reference here is particularly to the Gethsemane experience (Matt. 26:36-46). Our author conceives of Jesus as having been "heard for his godly fear" (vs. 7) on this occasion, a reference to the nature of Jesus' prayer, which was to the effect that his Father's will and not his own should be accomplished. The resignation of man's will to God is a fundamental characteristic of "godly fear" in the biblical sense of that term (Gen. 3:17; Heb. 3:16; 4:6, 11). That Jesus "learned obedience" through his sufferings is a characteristic teaching also of the Apostle Paul (Phil. 2:5-11).

The phrase "made perfect" (vs. 9) has the sense in the Greek of "having attained a previously determined goal." The meaning here is that Jesus obediently accepted the suffering which was laid upon him by the sinful condition of the world into which, at the Father's command, he had entered. The result of this utter obedience to his Father regardless of cost was our Lord's maturing to the point where he became worthy of being "the source of eternal salvation to all who obey him" (vs. 9). There is no indication in verse 10 of the point of time at which Jesus was "designated by God a high priest after the order of Melchizedek," but the logic of the author's argument would suggest that such designation was the result of the obedience and the consequent maturing process which has just been described. It has been suggested that God's

appointment of Jesus as High Priest came at the Ascension and
was synchronous with his entrance into the heavenly tabernacle.
Such a view, however, probably goes beyond the *chronological*
interest of the author. Rather, the *logical* sequence is what he is
concerned to stress here.

Qualifications of Mature Sons (5:11—6:20)

Teachers of the Word of Righteousness (5:11-14)

This long section (5:11—6:20) disrupts the author's description of the Son's high priesthood. Verse 10 is clearly repeated at
6:20, and thereafter the argument is taken up in chapter 7. This
is, however, in accordance with the author's general plan of ming-
ling hortatory with didactic sections in his letter. Further, it has
the effect once again of throwing into relief the contrast between
"Son" and "sons" which runs through the letter.

It is quite apparent from the description of the author's readers
that they are by no means new converts. Considerable time has
elapsed since they became Christians, and "by this time" they
should themselves have been ready to become teachers of others.
He is keenly disappointed to discover that again they require to
be taught "the first principles of God's word" (vs. 12). The word
translated "principles" here is the common Greek expression
equivalent to our English ABC's and was applied in similar
fashion to the rudiments of any branch of learning. The branch
here intended is in verse 11 called in the Greek simply "the word"
("much to say"). In verse 13 it becomes "the word of righteousness" and in 6:1, "the elementary doctrines of Christ" or, as the
Greek has it, "the elementary word of Christ." This is certainly
to be identified with "the message which they heard" (4:2) and
"the word of God" (4:12), and consequently with the gospel,
which was under discussion in chapters 3 and 4.

The message which the author says he is concerned to trans-
mit to his readers is "the word of righteousness" (vs. 13). This is
a word which, as he remarks, is fit not for a "child" but rather
"for the mature." His general meaning here is clear, but his use
of the qualifying phrase "of righteousness" is the more striking
inasmuch as it is not a common one in this letter. We have seen
the word "righteousness" thus far only in 1:9, where it was employed in connection with the description of the eternal Christ
who loves righteousness and hates iniquity. It is perhaps significant

that the next passage in which the word is used is at 7:2, where the author translates Melchizedek as "king of righteousness." Obviously teaching with regard to such a high priest might well be termed "the word of righteousness." But the author is also aware of "the righteousness which comes by faith" (11:7; 12:11). Moreover, the mature who are ready to receive such a word are those who, according to the author, "have their faculties trained by practice to distinguish good from evil." Perhaps, therefore, we should see in the use of the term here a reference to the total demand of God upon human life, which elsewhere in Scripture is termed "righteousness" (see Matt. 3:15).

Nonfulfillment by the Sons (6:1-8)

In this passage "the elementary doctrines of Christ" which the readers are exhorted to leave behind are basic theological doctrines which may be said to form a convenient summary of a well-rounded theology and may very well have constituted the substance of early catechetical teaching given to new converts. These, says our author, are merely the food of babes in Christ. The maturity, then, of which the author speaks (vs. 1) constitutes something for the Christian which, while based upon theology, goes beyond it. And we are left in no doubt as to what this further aspect of the Christian life is. For in verse 7 he presents us with a parable of a fruitful land which takes advantage of every gift of God's providence as it comes and "brings forth vegetation useful to those for whose sake it is cultivated." There can be no doubt that the fruitage which is suggested here is the Christian life and character which, in the teachings of both Jesus and Paul, are the natural fruitage of theological teaching and its associated spiritual experience (Matt. 5:16; Rom. 12:1-2; Gal. 5:22-25).

It is not without significance that the author in this section gives us two lists of the "elementary doctrines of Christ"—one of these a series of catechetical statements, as we have just remarked; the other a series of experiences had by the new convert. The first series, it will be noted, includes (1) those relating to the initial experiences of the Christian life: "repentance from dead works," "faith toward God," "instruction about ablutions," and "the laying on of hands"; and (2) those pertaining to the future: the "resurrection of the dead" and "eternal judgment" (vss. 1-2). The second series is intended to match this one with a list of experiences of which the readers are aware. In this series also perhaps we should see two sub-classes—(1) those pertaining to the initial experience of the Christian life: "repentance," enlightenment (a common synonym for baptism in the Early Church), tasting of "the heavenly gift," and becoming "partakers of the Holy Spirit," which perhaps should be equated with the "laying on of hands" above; and (2) those which relate to the realm of eschatology: the tasting of "the goodness of the word of God" and "the powers of the age to come" (vss. 4-5). It is not possible to push the similarity between the two lists to the point of exact parallelism. The author's desire is simply to warn his readers of the importance of advancing to maturity in their Christian lives.

This passage has been a great theological battleground. Some find in the passage proof of the doctrine of "backsliding," whereas others point out that the author specifically teaches that repentance after such presumptive backsliding is impossible. It should be noted, therefore, that the passage really suits neither group. On the one hand, it may be suggested that the "apostasy" referred to in verse 6 is a hypothetical one, found in a hortatory passage, and intended merely as a warning to the readers (see also vs. 8). On the other hand, it is to be remarked that the author only says that "it is impossible to restore again to repentance" such as continually crucify the Son of God ("since they crucify the Son of God"). The tense of the Greek verb here suggests that, "as long as men crucify the Son of God on their own account and hold him up to contempt," they are not in a condition to repent.

In this passage, as previously (1:1-4), it is clear that for the author two ages overlap. Christians already to some extent are living in the "age to come" and experiencing its powers (vs. 5), while the works of which they have repented are those pertaining to the sphere of death (vs. 1), particularly those of a ritualistic nature attaching to the old cult (9:14). It is this contact with the coming age and the powers which pertain to it that arouses the expectancy of the author that his Christian readers may indeed advance to maturity. This idea is explicitly brought out in the next section.

Guaranteed by God Through His High-Priestly Son (6:9-20)

It was noted above that the "apostasy" against which our author warned his readers was of a hypothetical nature (vss. 4-6). That this is true so far as the author's readers are concerned is now made doubly clear by his words in verse 9—"in your case, beloved, we feel sure of better things that belong to salvation" (see also 10:39). It may seem strange that he can both utter such words of assurance and in no uncertain terms warn his readers of the dangers of apostasy. And yet Christians always stand in such a position of jeopardy while in the world of human affairs. Like the father at the foot of the Mount of Transfiguration they are constrained to cry out, "I believe," and then in the next half breath, "help my unbelief!" (Mark 9:24). The Christian walk is always to be expressed both in the indicative mood and in the mood of command or entreaty. Paul gives ample expression to these two features in Romans 6:2-11.

In the present instance the two factors referred to are clearly evidenced in our author's argument. First, corresponding to the "I believe" or indicative statement of the case for the Christian, our author calls attention to "your work and the love which you showed for his sake in serving the saints, as you still do" (vs. 10). The "work" referred to here is not to be confused with "good works" under the Law. As we have seen, our author refers to those as "dead works," that is, works which are not characterized by the life or living character experienced by the saved (vs. 1; 9:14). This "work" is rather the product of the Christian's experience of the Holy Spirit and "the powers of the age to come" which he has already mentioned (vss. 4 and 5). The "love" to which he refers is intended as a further definition of "your work," the two expressions used together to express a single idea. This brotherly love must have been a particularly strong characteristic of the community addressed in this letter, as the author refers to it again (13:1).

But the second factor—the need for an imperative—is also applicable to the readers' condition. For there is a "hope" which still lies ahead (vs. 11). This hope is akin to, if not identical with, the old "promises" of God to his people under the Old Covenant (vs. 12). Accordingly, "earnestness in realizing the full assurance of hope" and in becoming "imitators of those who through faith and patience inherit the promises" is called for.

The four words which stand out in connection with this side of the matter are obviously "faith," "patience," "promises," and "hope." Individually and collectively these four words serve to stress the fact that in the last analysis salvation lies with God and is guaranteed by him alone. Left to themselves, the "sons" are unable to fulfill the qualifications demanded of the mature. This is the work of God accomplished through his high-priestly Son.

Indeed, it is now apparent that the Christian life must be represented as an ellipse whose two foci are respectively the Cross (2:9) and the Second Coming (9:28). These represent in temporal terms the past and future redemptive activity of God, its historical and eternal aspects. In the present section the author is concerned to stress particularly the future focus of the Christian life (vss. 18-20).

"Hope" in this author's vocabulary is by no means a weak affair. Rather it is a veritable "anchor of the soul." It is an objective reality, not merely a subjective whim. It is the very work of Christ as he presents his sacrificed body before God in the eternal sanctuary. The language of this passage ("inner shrine," "curtain," "high priest") plunges us into the midst of a new subject which goes far beyond the foundation thus far laid down. Further explanation, therefore, must await such passages as 8:1-5 and 9: 11-14.

To illustrate the sense in which he employs the terms "faith," "patience" or endurance, and "promises," the author cites the case of Abraham and the incident of his offering of Isaac on Mount Moriah (Gen. 22:16-17), in which, although the elements of faith and patience on Abraham's part are not overlooked, the emphasis is clearly upon God's part in the transaction. The author lays great stress upon the fact that the promise came from God to begin with and rested upon his employing an "oath" to seal the promise. These two, promise and oath, are "unchangeable things, in which it is impossible that God should prove false" (vs. 18). The argument here is essentially the same as that found in chapters 3 and 4, in which "the promise of entering his rest," which God had originally made through Moses and Joshua to the people of Israel, must remain open for some future generation to receive, for the reason that when God promises he always fulfills.

Essentially, then, the teaching of this section is that, although the readers have not yet attained to the maturity required of sons, one may rest assured that they will do so—not because of any power residing within themselves, but because of the determined purpose of God and the fulfillment of that purpose through the work of Jesus Christ. As "forerunner" (vs. 20) Jesus has run on ahead into the presence of God on our behalf. He is accordingly the "pioneer" of the Christian faith, and as he has planted the "anchor" of our hope within the eternal sanctuary, he is the "perfecter of our faith," that is, he has brought to fulfillment our promised salvation.

The Son's Melchizedekian High Priesthood (7:1-28)

Supremacy of the Melchizedekian High Priesthood (7:1-10)

The author now comes to deal in a conclusive fashion with the supremacy of the Melchizedekian high priesthood over that of the Levitical order. And by implication the Son of God who, according to Hebrews, belongs to the Melchizedekian order will share in this supremacy. The author appears to argue from Melchizedek to Christ. But in reality he intends his argument to proceed in the other direction, for in verse 3 he speaks of Melchizedek as "resembling the Son of God." It is probably correct to say that he has chosen Melchizedek merely because the description of him and his office found in Genesis 14:17-20 and Psalm 110:4 serves his present purpose. The major point which he wishes to make is that the high-priestly or sacrificial work of Christ has superseded all the sacrifices offered under the Levitical order.

Melchizedek's very name and title suggested his close association with God's saving purpose for man. For "righteousness" ("zedek") and "peace" ("Salem") were two of the words commonly employed by the Hebrew prophets to refer to God's redemptive activity (vs. 2). Melchizedek, therefore, as a redemptive figure might very appropriately be employed as a foil for Jesus Christ, God's ultimate redemptive agent in the world.

Hebrews suggests three senses in which Melchizedek is to be thought of as superior. Of these the first is the most important, and it is this one in which the author finds particular (perhaps one should say exclusive) likeness to Jesus Christ. This is the fact that in the Genesis record Melchizedek is apparently "without father or mother or genealogy, and has neither beginning of days nor end of life" (vs. 3). It is true that in Genesis, Melchizedek is not described in these terms. The author of Hebrews is basing his argument upon the well-known fact that it was customary for the author of Genesis, upon introducing any great figure, to state his genealogy (see Gen. 5 for Noah; 11 for Abraham). Melchizedek, as we read his story in Genesis, is an obvious exception to this rule. He flashes, so to speak, across the stage of history like a meteor. He arrives without announcement, without pedigree, without fanfare of any sort. And having done the work which God gave him to do, he flashes off into the night again. The author sees him in this respect as like Jesus Christ, who came out of eternity in the Incarnation, performed his appointed service in a short span of years, and by his resurrection and ascension again passed out into the eternal order. Of each of these, therefore, it may be said that "he continues a priest for ever" (vs. 3). For where there is neither beginning nor ending, it may be argued that there is only continuity in the priestly office.

The second feature which places Melchizedek above the Levitical order is the fact that according to the Genesis account "Abraham the patriarch gave him a tithe of the spoils" (vs. 4). The Mosaic Law declared that only those belonging to the tribe of Levi were to receive tithes (Num. 18:21). But it would appear that Abraham recognized in Melchizedek a transcendent figure worthy of receiving tithes, not because this was validated by a law but because of his inherent worth. Moreover, it could be argued from the Jewish point of view that all Levitical priests, who were so to speak "still in the loins" (vs. 10) of Abraham, had by his action conceded the right of Melchizedek to receive tithes even from themselves! Such an argument may not appeal to us, but there is no question that it would be acceptable among those accustomed to rabbinical methods of logic and interpretation of the Scriptures. The argument was based upon the assumption that a degree of continuity is found in the successive generations of men throughout history—a continuity which results in a certain corporate responsibility and privilege. This principle was allowed by the Jew in the day in which our author wrote, and indeed it has a certain legitimacy attaching to it for any day. It is simply a matter of common observation that what is done by one generation is done for all succeeding generations. The achievements and mistakes made by one generation accrue to the credit or debit of all which follow.

Hebrews' third argument in favor of Melchizedek's superiority to the Levitical order is found in the fact that "Melchizedek . . . met Abraham . . . and blessed him" (vs. 1). But it is a matter of common knowledge that "the inferior is blessed by the superior" (vs. 7). Melchizedek accordingly, it may be argued, is superior both to Abraham and to the Levitical priesthood in his loins. Here again is an argument drawn from the facts as stated in Genesis which is sufficiently cogent to justify our author's choice of Mel-

chizedek as a type of Christ. For it is true that the greater blesses
the lesser. And again our author's argument will mean in the last
analysis that Melchizedek receives a priesthood from God which
guarantees its own validity. This priest needs no law to justify his
blessing the greatest man of God in his day. This right to bless is
inherent in the office which Melchizedek has received from God.
Man can neither add to nor subtract from the validity of such a
right.

There is even some historical justification for the choice of
Melchizedek as the proper figure preceding the Levitical priesthood to typify our Lord as Messiah-High Priest. The "Salem" of
which Melchizedek was king-priest was generally acknowledged
to be the predecessor of Jerusalem, which was built presumably
on the same site (see Ps. 76:2). It could be argued, therefore,
that David and his successors of Jerusalem had succeeded to the
high-priestly functions of Melchizedek of Salem and, as Jesus
himself pointed out, David as the "messiah" of God considered
himself as having been given priestly prerogatives (Mark 2:26).
The psalmist in Psalm 110:1 is doubtless drawing upon this tradition in declaring the king of Israel to be at once messiah and high
priest of God. And the author of Hebrews, in taking over and
applying Psalm 110 to Jesus Christ—an act which is no doubt
based on Jesus' own teaching in Mark 12:36 (see 5:6 above)—
has done no more than the Early Church would have considered
legitimate. For that Church, Jesus Christ was the fulfillment of
all types and promises made under the Old Covenant. As Prophet,
Priest, and King he combined within his own function all of the
prophetic, priestly, and kingly ministries of his people.

Suspension of the Levitical Order (7:11-22)

The author now attempts to show that it was right and proper
that the Levitical priesthood should be superseded by the Melchizedekian one. For "perfection" for man was obviously not
obtained under the Levitical priesthood and the Mosaic Law (vs.
11). This proves their general "weakness and uselessness" (vs.
18). "The law made nothing perfect" (vs. 19).

"Perfection" in this context and in succeeding ones (see 9:9;
10:1; 11:40; 12:23) would seem to have reference to the prepara-
tion of the spirit of man for fellowship with and worship of God.
And the author's argument is that this cannot be accomplished by
law or by a priesthood established by law. Rather it is to be

achieved only by that act of Jesus Christ as the great High Priest to which we have already been introduced (6:19-20), namely, the planting of the anchor of the Christian hope firmly upon the mercy seat in the eternal sanctuary.

In the course of this argument the author finds it necessary to establish the fact that the Levitical priesthood has indeed been set aside through the changing of the Law (vs. 12). This he proves, first, by reminding his readers of the well-known fact that Jesus "belonged to another tribe" than Levi, a tribe "from which no one has ever served at the altar." This tribe was of course that of Judah (vss. 13-14). Second, he sets beside this historical fact the words of Psalm 110:4, in which the reigning messianic king is addressed as "priest for ever, after the order of Melchizedek" (vss. 15-17). The argument here is based upon the natural observation that the creation of a messiah-high priest after the order of Melchizedek which the Psalm avers, does not proceed upon the basis of law but rather contravenes the explicit commandment in the Law (vs. 18). It also assumes that there is in the Psalm an overtone reaching beyond the immediate messianic king and attaching itself to Jesus Christ, the eternal Son of God. The justification for this assumption on the author's part lies in his belief that Jesus had heard his Father speaking to him in these terms (see 5:6 and Mark 12:36). That Jesus Christ is such a High Priest justifies the setting aside of the Law regarding priests, a fact that rests upon "the power of an indestructible life" (vs. 16) which, as we have already seen, was his (vss. 3 and 8).

Finally, the author, as though to clinch his entire argument for the greater worth and validity of the Melchizedekian priesthood represented by Jesus, calls attention to the fact that in the Psalm the appointment of the messiah-high priest is made by God, under oath (vss. 20-22). This, as he rightly remarks, cannot be said of the Levitical priesthood. The very solemnity therefore by which the Melchizedekian priest is appointed is itself proof of his greater worth in the sight of God. Once again applying the words of the Psalm to Jesus Christ, he remarks, "This makes Jesus the surety of a better covenant" (vs. 22), thereby introducing a new element, that of the New Covenant. As we have already seen, it is this author's custom to introduce a new subject upon which he will expound at length later in the book. The theme will be developed particularly in chapters 8 and 9.

Characteristics of the Son as Melchizedekian High Priest (7:23-28)

In the closing verses of the seventh chapter the author takes the phrase "for ever" ("permanently" in vs. 24) from Psalm 110:4 and develops its meaning and application in the light of the eternal nature of the Son of God. His intention is to give assurance to the readers that their High Priest is able really "to save those who draw near to God through him" (vs. 25). This assurance is based upon the fact that Jesus Christ is an eternal figure who lives forever "to make intercession" for his people. By contrast the Levitical priests were many in number because death intervened to disrupt their priesthood; thus no assurance could be given that they would see matters through to a definitive end.

No doubt we should see a contrast between the phrases "for ever" (vs. 24, literally, "into eternity") and "for all time" (vs. 25), the one phrase referring to the eternal nature of the High Priest, Jesus Christ, and the other to the effectiveness of his work within time. His high priesthood is carried on in eternity, as we shall see carefully elaborated in the next chapter (8:1, 4), but its effectiveness is experienced also by the people whom he serves on the temporal plane. On that temporal plane and within history this High Priest had once offered himself on the cross (9:12; 10:10). But that one high-priestly act having been performed on the plane of history, the High Priest's further activity in the eternal order consists in "intercession" for his people (vs. 25).

And now we arrive at the pinnacle of Hebrews' characterization of this eternal High Priest, Jesus Christ. In verses 26-28 he is described in terms intended to set him apart from "those high priests" who officiate under the Levitical system. The author has already called attention to the fact that in his humanity the Levitical high priest was one with his people, inasmuch as he was "bound to offer sacrifice for his own sins as well as for those of the people" (5:3). This weakness of the Levitical high priest is here repeated (7:27). The suggestion that those high priests had to "offer sacrifices daily" is a pardonable use of hyperbole; the high priest was obliged to officiate only on one day of the Jewish calendar—the Day of Atonement. Nonetheless, his services on the Day of Atonement were intended to sum up all the sacrifices offered throughout the year previous, in order that, so to speak, the cultic worship might have its slate wiped clean and be enabled to start anew.

As the author indicates, however, Jesus as High Priest "did this once for all when he offered up himself," that is, upon the cross (vs. 27). For the Christian faith, then, the work of its High Priest, Jesus Christ, is as final as the Jewish Day of Atonement was conceived to be under the older faith. Only in this case no repetition of the high-priestly act is required year by year, and this essentially because of Jesus' eternal character as "a Son." This Son, it is true, had to be "made perfect for ever" (vs. 28), and this he became, as already noted, when "he learned obedience through what he suffered" (5:8); for, being thus "made perfect he became the source of eternal salvation to all who obey him" (5:9).

As previously remarked, in Hebrews the Christian life is considered as an ellipse with its two foci of Christ's death on the cross and his final coming. Each of these foci has one temporal event in view, and between them lies the activity of this eternal High Priest in the heavenly tabernacle (see chs. 8-10). This means, in effect, that the Atonement on the cross within history is an act of the eternal High Priest accomplished in the outer priestly court of the eternal tabernacle. This tabernacle has, so to speak, an outer court which crosses the line dividing history from eternity, and it is in this outer court in history that the Cross, or altar of Christian sacrifice, stands. Once the eternal High Priest, the Son of God, performs his sacrifice at that outer altar he immediately passes into the eternal tabernacle, never again being required to offer sacrifice for the sins of his people.

It would be a mistake to understand from verse 27 that the author thinks of Jesus as offering sacrifice even once "for his own sins." This might be inferred from the fact that he goes on to say that "he did this once for all when he offered up himself." But the high terms which he uses to describe the character of Jesus Christ as the eternal Son and the eternal High Priest preclude any such conclusion. In the present context he speaks of him rather as "holy, blameless, unstained, separated from sinners, exalted above the heavens" (vs. 26). And elsewhere in the letter he will allow no more than that Jesus himself "has suffered and been tempted" (2:18), that "he learned obedience through what he suffered" (5:8), and that he was "one who in every respect has been tempted as we are, yet without sinning" (4:15). This is also the unanimous testimony of the New Testament Scriptures regarding the Church's belief in the sinless character of its Lord (Matt. 4:1-11; John 8:46; II Cor. 5:21).

THE EFFICACY OF THE SON'S HIGH-PRIESTLY WORK

Hebrews 8:1—10:18

Summary Statement (8:1-6)

The Greek word translated "the point" may mean either "principal point," "summary," or even "crown"; and similarly the phrase translated "in what we are saying" may be taken to mean generally the argument of the letter as a whole, or rather to refer to what has previously been said, or even to what is about to be said. Inasmuch as in these six verses the author introduces a reference successively to the sacrifice, tabernacle, and covenant as they relate to the high-priestly work of the Son of God—matters not previously mentioned at all, or if so only in casual fashion, and about to be developed in the next two and a half chapters—we shall assume that the intention here is to give a summary statement of the argument about to be presented.

In general the teaching of the passage is clear enough. Returning to Psalm 110:1 (see 1:13), the author begins with an inclusive statement intended to define the twofold function of the Son of God as High Priest and Messianic King "seated at the right hand of the throne of the Majesty in heaven" (vs. 1). It is not without significance that, whereas the theme of our Lord's high priesthood is never lost sight of in chapters 5 through 11, his Messianic office is referred to only at the beginning of the argument (1:3, 13), at the beginning and end of the discussion regarding his high-priestly work (8:1; 10:12-13), and at 12:2, where the purpose is to exhort the readers to endurance or steadfastness. Jesus Christ is able to call into action the whole divine power to save. For this is what it means to be "seated at the right hand of the throne of the Majesty in heaven."

The summary statement involves a triple contrast between (1) the "true tent" or tabernacle (vs. 2) which this High Priest serves, as over against the "copy and shadow of the heavenly sanctuary" served by the Levitical high priesthood (vs. 5); (2) the "gifts and sacrifices" offered under the two orders (vs. 3); and (3) the "covenant" which is declared to be better than the first covenant of the Old Testament period (vs. 6).

The first of these three contrasts concerns the nature of the tabernacle employed in the worship of the old and new faiths. Quoting from the Greek translation of Exodus 25:40, the author points out that the original tabernacle employed by Moses in the wilderness had been made "according to the pattern which was shown . . . [him] on the mountain" (vs. 5), and that in consequence it was merely "a copy and shadow of the heavenly sanctuary." By contrast, therefore, our author sees the heavenly tabernacle served by our Lord as the "true" one, or, in other words, the original or "pattern" of that served by Moses.

The second contrast which Hebrews makes between the old and the new systems of worship concerns the matter of "gifts and sacrifices" (vs. 3). This theme the author will develop at length in chapter 9. For the moment he abandons it with the mere suggestion that "it is necessary" that Jesus Christ as High Priest also "have something to offer." And then he curiously inserts at this point (vs. 4) a statement which appears to be out of place insofar as his immediate argument is concerned. Perhaps we should see here a statement intentionally directed against the teaching of the Qumran sect. For so far as our evidence goes, they alone among contemporary Jews believed in a messiah-high priest, or a messiah proceeding from among the sons of Aaron (see Introduction). In Hebrews the High Priest is also Messiah (that is, "one who is seated at the right hand of the throne of the Majesty in heaven" vs. 1), but with the differences that he is not a descendant of Aaron and is Son of God.

The third contrast between the old and new ministries is that pertaining to the nature of the two Covenants involved (vs. 6). And for the moment our author contents himself with the statement that the New Covenant "is enacted on better promises" than the Old. In passing, it should be observed that reference is made here to *only one* "old" Covenant. This is in accord with the Jewish point of view and that of the Hebrew prophets. For according to that old Hebrew-Jewish view there was but one Covenant which God made with his people, beginning with Abraham. The one Covenant was repeated many times—to Isaac, to Jacob, to Israel at the Exodus, and on numerous other occasions. But the Covenant was one, whatever the immediate promises involved might be.

What the "better promises" are which attach to the New Covenant are not here specified. And in fact this theme is nowhere fully developed in the letter. We are left merely with such a pas-

sage as 10:23 and the preceding verses 19-22 from which to in-
fer that the promises intended have reference to our confident entering of "the sanctuary by the blood of Jesus." Indeed, in the
final analysis there is no difference between the promises attaching to Old and New Covenants. This the author himself makes clear
at 11:39-40. The promises attaching to the New Covenant can
only be better, therefore, in the sense that Jesus Christ as High
Priest actually *fulfills* in his person and work all the promises
which God ever gives to his people throughout history.

Ineffectiveness of the Old Covenant (8:7—9:10)

The Old Covenant (8:7-13)

The author's thesis at this point is clearly expressed in verses 7
and 13—the "first covenant" was not "faultless" and therefore became "obsolete." Being essentially inferior and outworn, the
time had come for the Old Covenant to "vanish away." This, of
course, gave room for the coming of "a new covenant," the one
under which the great High Priest Jesus Christ functions.

In proof of the inferior and "obsolete" nature of the first
Covenant the author turns to the prophetic Scriptures. Jeremiah
(31:31-34) had foreseen the day when the Lord who had made
a first Covenant with Israel would make another of quite different
nature (see also Ezek. 36:24-32). The passage from Jeremiah
adequately meets the needs of our author, inasmuch as the New
Covenant which it prophesies is to be "not like the covenant that I
made with their fathers" (vs. 9). That one had been given to the
people as a whole and was written upon tables of stone. This one
by contrast was to be characterized by laws written upon the
"minds" and "hearts" of men (vs. 10). Nor was the Covenant
made with the people as an undivided unit; rather, it was made in
a manner to take account of individual needs and requirements,
so that it should not be necessary for one to teach another the
knowledge of the Lord, "for all shall know me, from the least of
them to the greatest" (vs. 11).

Though the teaching of the passage is clear, several points may
advisedly find comment. First, the nature of a "covenant" in the
biblical sense should be noted. The very words employed in the
scriptural languages denote something quite different from the
Latin, from which our English word is derived. In Latin and English the word "covenant" means a mutual agreement made by two

equal parties who meet together to settle a dispute between them. The Hebrew and Greek words, on the contrary, might better be translated "a divine disposal" or "a sovereign proposal." In Scripture a covenant in which God and man are concerned refers to a plan which God has conceived and by which man is required to live his life. Man is free merely to accept or reject God's Covenant; he cannot in any particular alter it or state conditions for its functioning. Second, it is clear to both Jeremiah and the author of Hebrews that only two Covenants are to be recognized in Scripture, both made by God with the people of his choice. If the Old Covenant is worthless and "obsolete," it is God who recognizes that this is the case and who makes his plans for the establishment of a New Covenant. Third, it is not a matter of concern to the author of Hebrews that the passage from Jeremiah states that the "new covenant" is to be made "with the house of Israel and with the house of Judah" (vs. 8). For the author, as for the Early Church generally (see Rom. 9:6; Gal. 6:16; I Peter 1:1-2; Rev. 7:4), the Christian community itself is that "Israel" (or "Judah") to which the prophet refers. In this respect as in others, we see that there is similarity and yet dissimilarity between the teaching of Hebrews and that of the Qumran sect. For that sect also held that it was the people of the "new covenant." It is as though the author of Hebrews were declaring that the Christian Church and not the Qumran community constitutes the true people of God with whom God has made a New Covenant through Jesus Christ. Finally, it is declared that, with this New Covenant, God will be "merciful toward their iniquities" and he "will remember their sins no more" (vs. 12). In other words, the aim of true religion will now be accomplished—the achievement of real fellowship between God and man, fellowship no longer disrupted by the remembrance of sin, that stumbling block which in the beginning disrupted the fellowship (Gen. 3:22-24; Heb. 3:16-19).

The Old Tabernacle (9:1-5)

The author, by implication, has already dealt a telling blow to the effectiveness of the old Tabernacle by speaking of it as merely "a copy and shadow of the heavenly sanctuary" (8:5). He now describes this Tabernacle with a view to pointing out certain features which suggest its "obsolete" nature.

With some detail he describes, and quite accurately indeed, the construction and furniture of the "earthly sanctuary" which traditionally had been set up by Moses in the wilderness and which is generally called the "tabernacle" (vs. 2, see margin) to distinguish it from the Temple (Solomon's, Zerubbabel's, and Herod's). For its description of the sanctuary Hebrews depends upon Exodus 25 and 26, according to which it was divided into two tabernacles or tents, in the first ("outer one") of which were to be found "the lampstand and the table and the bread of the Presence." This tent (called "the Holy Place") also contained the golden altar of incense, although as the author suggests, this golden altar actually pertained to "the Holy of Holies" or inner tent (vss. 3-5). The purpose of the golden altar was for burning the incense which arose like a sweet savor and passed over the "second curtain" and so into the Holy of Holies and before the "mercy seat" (see Exod. 30:1-10). In the Holy of Holies was "the ark of the covenant," which, according to one tradition at least, contained the historic items listed in verse 4. We should probably understand that the "cherubim of glory" stood on either side of the Ark and spread their wings over the "mercy seat" or representation of God's throne which formed the cover of the Ark (see Exod. 25:10-22).

"Of these things," the author remarks, "we cannot now speak in detail" (vs. 5). Such details as he mentions are merely to show that "the first covenant had regulations for worship" which were adapted to its function (vs. 1). It is only as we pass on into the next section (vss. 6-10) that we discover the author's motive in representing the details of the sanctuary as he has done. His argument has reference to the presence of "the second curtain" (vs. 3) hung between the Holy Place and the Holy of Holies. And his point is that as long as this division existed between the two tents or tabernacles, there could be no real fellowship between God and man.

The question has long been debated as to why Hebrews nowhere mentions Herod's Temple as standing on Mount Zion in Jerusalem but rather chooses, for purpose of comparison between the Old Covenant and the New, to speak of the Tabernacle set up in the wilderness. It has been argued that this is evidence of the late date of the letter, which on this assumption was not written until well after the destruction of Jerusalem with its Temple in A.D. 70. This argument, however, is no longer valid; Judaism had already, before the First Jewish War (A.D. 66-70), begun to break away from the Temple worship in Jerusalem. Sometime after the Exile,

the synagogue had sprung up, particularly under the influence of
the Pharisees and their rabbis, and had become the real center of
worship for the average Jew. Also, the Qumran sect, whether at
its central monastery at Khirbet Qumran or in its numerous scattered communities or "encampments," refused to support the worship of the Temple, at least to the extent of offering sacrifices
there. But this animus toward the Temple and its sacrifices did
not carry over to the Tabernacle, which, unlike the Temple, had
the prestige of the Mosaic Law behind it (Exod. chs. 25-40). In
view of these facts it is not surprising that the Letter to the Hebrews should center its thought upon the Tabernacle in the wilderness. No Jew of the day could fail to acknowledge its legitimacy,
and in holding it up for criticism the author therefore was striking
at the very heart of worship under the Old Covenant.

The Old Sacrifices (9:6-10)

Hebrews now proceeds to show the inadequacy of the sacrifices
offered in the Tabernacle according to the terms of the Old Covenant. It is true, the author says, that the Levitical "priests go continually into the outer tent, performing their ritual duties" (vs.
6). But he sees the utmost significance attaching to the fact that
these priests in their daily rounds are not permitted to enter into
the Holy of Holies. Only the high priest is allowed to enter there
"and he but once a year" (vs. 7; see Lev. 16:2, 14, 29-34).

The "ritual duties" (vs. 6) which the common priests were allowed to perform in the Holy Place included the burning of incense on the golden altar, the placing of shewbread, and the
lighting of the seven lights of the "lampstand." But the "second"
curtain dividing the Holy Place from the Holy of Holies debarred
them from entrance to the very presence of God as signified by
the mercy seat on the Ark of the Covenant. The author sees in
the existence of this curtain an indication by the "Holy Spirit"
that "the way into the sanctuary is not yet opened as long as the
outer tent is still standing" (vs. 8). That is, there can be no con-
tinual fellowship between God and his people as long as this curtain exists. It is true, as we have already seen (5:3; 7:27), that the
high priest once a year is allowed to enter the Holy of Holies with
a view to sprinkling the "blood" in that tent and even upon the
Ark of the Covenant itself, blood "which he offers for himself
and for the errors of the people" (vs. 7; Lev. 16:11-19). But even
if this sprinkling of blood were conceded to have accomplished

the end in view, yet it is obvious that such single contact would have done little for the cause of true religion. It is with this little, however, that the author is vitally concerned, for it is the product of the high priest's work on the Day of Atonement. And it is the work of the high priests under the two Covenants which, by and large, he wishes to compare (vss. 11-14). It is to be remembered, however, that in theory all the sacrifices of the Jewish year reached their climax and were subsumed in those offered by the high priest on the Day of Atonement. The author considers the existence of the "second curtain" as "symbolic for the present age" (vs. 9). Putting together all the sacrifices and offerings under the Old Covenant, he holds that neither singly nor collectively do they accomplish the end in view. That is, they "cannot perfect the conscience of the worshiper." They do not bring to maturity man's awareness of fellowship with God, nor can they prepare his spirit to be worthy of such fellowship. Rather, Hebrews sees them as merely "ritual duties" (vs. 6), that is, as ceremonials whose function is to keep alive the cult and to carry on its ritual from year to year. They "deal only with food and drink and various ablutions, regulations for the body" (vs. 10). They serve to cleanse the worshiper and the instruments and furniture of worship and are performed in accordance with the various taboos of a cult religion. Looked at from this point of view, even the work of the high priest on the Day of Atonement is nothing more than a cultic act or series of acts whose sole purpose is to sum up the necessary cultic acts prescribed for a given year, with a view to starting a new religious year afresh. And indeed it may be said that the ritual enjoined in Leviticus 16, in which the high priest sprinkles the blood of the appointed sacrifices upon all the furniture of worship, the Tabernacle itself in its various parts, and even the worshiping congregation, appears to justify the conclusion of the author. Such cultic acts are "imposed until the time of reformation" (vs. 10) or of transformation, which, of course, Hebrews equates with the Christian era.

Effectiveness of the New Covenant (9:11-28)

The New Sacrifice (9:11-14)

The few verses of the present section represent the heart of the message of Hebrews. Sacrifice with a view to the assurance of the worshiper's acceptance into fellowship with God is, on different levels, the high point of religion in both the Old and New Scriptures. As we have just seen, this high point was supposed to have been reached once a year on the Day of Atonement with the entrance of the high priest into the Holy of Holies. The concern of the present section, therefore, is to show that, whereas the sacrifices which the Jewish high priest presented on that occasion were inadequate to serve spiritual ends, by contrast the sacrifice of Jesus Christ as eternal High Priest did accomplish these very ends. The author summarizes in these few verses much that he has already said. Indeed, almost every word of the passage is full of meaning—meaning either previously pointed out or now for the first time disclosed. This may be briefly summarized as follows:

First, the stress falls on the high priesthood of Jesus Christ, a conception which has been a major point of the letter from 2:17 forward. Here the high priesthood is defined as relating to "the good things that have come" (vs. 11), or that have happened.

Second, Christ's high-priestly work includes his traversing "the greater and more perfect tent (not made with hands, that is, not of this creation)." This is in contrast to the functioning of both high priest and lesser priests of the Jewish cult to which reference was made in verses 6-10. The point had already been made at 4:14 that "we have a great high priest who has passed through the heavens, Jesus, the Son of God." That is to say, our Lord has high-priestly functions in the eternal and genuine tabernacle, a fact to which further reference will be made in verses 24-28.

Third, the offering which he has to make is "not the blood of goats and calves but his own blood" (vs. 12), and therefore it is an offering worthy of "securing an eternal redemption" for the people of God. The offering of blood on the part of Christ is to be understood in the light of: (1) the act of the Jewish high priest on the Day of Atonement, who sprinkled the blood of a bull (Lev. 16:14) and of a goat (Lev. 16:15-19) on the mercy seat in the Holy of Holies to make atonement for the sins of all the people; (2) the next passage (9:15-22), where the blood is explained as being "the blood of the covenant" (vs. 20); and (3) those passages in Hebrews in which Christ's offering is said to be that of "himself" (9:14, 25) or his "body" (10:10-12; see 9:28). From a study of all these passages it becomes clear that "blood," when shed and presented to God, stands for the dedication of the life, the giving of all that can be rendered on behalf of man.

Fourth, the author clinches his argument with a reference to

the efficacy of the sacrifices offered on the Day of Atonement by
the Jewish high priest. Far from denying that efficacy, he asserts
it as the basis of his argument for the validity and efficacy of the
sacrifice of Christ. He asserts, however, that the sacrifices of the
Jewish sacrificial system avail only "for the purification of the
flesh" (vs. 13), that is, only for the purposes of the cultic system
of worship, as we have already seen above in verses 9 and 10.
Here he mentions specifically "the blood of goats and bulls" because it was such blood as this that the high priest offered on the
Day of Atonement (Lev. 16:11-19). As already said above, the
only sacrifices and rituals to which reference is made in Hebrews
are those which concern the activity of the high priest on the Day
of Atonement. This is because the author is concerned to compare
Christ as eternal High Priest with the high priest under the Levitical system, but also because the sacrifices performed by the high
priest on that day were in a real sense climactic and may be considered as embracing all others under the Mosaic Law. The only
exception to this statement is perhaps the reference to "the ashes
of a heifer" (vs. 13). These ashes had nothing specifically to do
with the work of the high priest nor with the sacrifices of the Day
of Atonement. They were employed in connection with the purification of a person who had touched a corpse (Num. 19:9, 17-19).
They do, therefore, have a general reference to the subject in
hand, inasmuch as an unclean person was excluded from the fellowship and particularly from the worship of the people of God.
And the point of this letter is exactly that the work of Christ accomplishes all that is necessary in order to achieve this end.

Finally, "the blood of Christ" stands for his self-offering through
"the eternal Spirit" (vs. 14). That is to say, the guarantor of
Christ's sacrifice is not an ephemeral animal, but rather is the
eternal Spirit of God. Christ's act, therefore, is an act efficacious
in the realm of spirit and should be of service to all those who
would purify the "conscience from dead works" with a view to
serving the God who is alive (vs. 14; see vs. 9).

The New Covenant (9:15-23)

The author now returns to a comparison of the covenants pertaining to the two religions which he is contrasting. His argument
takes the form of a series of illustrations designed to prove that
no covenant is properly ratified without the shedding of blood.
The first of these is taken from the custom of drafting a last "will"

and testament (vs. 16). In the Greek the same term is employed
for a "covenant" and for a "will." Playing upon this double usage
of the word in Greek, the author can remark that "the death of
the one who made it [the will] must be established. For a will
takes effect only at death, since it is not in force as long as the one
who made it is alive" (vss. 16-17). Paul makes a somewhat similar
use of the double connotation of the word in Galatians 3:15
(see margin).

The second illustration, taken from the ratification of the first
Covenant in the time of Moses, is more obviously relevant (vss.
18-21). In his account of the matter the author has curiously
mixed together several passages (Exod. 24:3-8; 12:22; Lev. 8:15,
19; Num. 19:6) which had severally to do with the ratification
of the first Covenant, the celebration of the Passover at the Exodus, and the purification of a leper. Whether this is intentional on
his part or simply a matter of inadvertence, we have no way of
knowing. He also remarks in verse 19 that "the book itself"—presumably the "book of the covenant" (Exod. 24:7)—is sprinkled
with the blood of the Covenant, but of this there is no evidence
in the original account. Further, he says that "the tent and all the
vessels used in worship" were sprinkled with the blood (vs. 21),
although there was no Tabernacle until later.

The third illustration which the author employs is of a more
general character, as he makes the sweeping statement that "under
the law almost everything is purified with blood" (vs. 22). This
statement is correct, and the various purifications by blood on the
Day of Atonement are the best proof of the same.

The author now concludes that since "the copies" are cleansed
with blood, "the heavenly things themselves" require to be cleansed
with "better sacrifices" (vs. 23). The argument is, of course, an
analogical one and can carry us only so far. It is based, as is the
whole argument of Hebrews with regard to Christ's high priesthood, upon a fundamental belief in the continuity of revelation
between the Old and New Covenants. In consequence we must
believe the readers to be Jewish Christians for whom the Old
Testament Scriptures constituted an authoritative document before they accepted the Christian faith. The author now reverts in
verse 15 to what he has already said with regard to "those who
are called" to "receive the promised eternal inheritance," which
is the theme of the gospel whenever it is uttered. It is obvious, too,
that it is particularly to such Jewish Christians that his statement

would be peculiarly of interest that "a death has occurred which redeems them from the transgressions under the first covenant" (vs. 15). "Redemption" literally refers to the manumission of slaves and in the scriptural context always recalls the redemption of Israel from the bondage of slavery in Egypt. No Jewish Christian could fail so to understand the reference. However, in the New Testament Scriptures the word has undergone a distinct spiritualization and generally refers, as here, to the forgiveness of sins (Eph. 1:7; Col. 1:14; see Rom. 3:24-26). Thus it would be clear, at any rate to those who had the teachings of the Hebrew prophetic Scriptures in mind and who were acquainted with the analogies presented by the author, that the second Covenant could accomplish what the first Covenant merely foreshadowed; and indeed this accomplishment included forgiveness of transgressions which the Law under the first Covenant had multiplied (see Rom. 5:20-21).

The New Tabernacle (9:24-28)

In dividing chapters 8 and 9 into various sections, we must avoid every tendency to limit the author's discussion in any section to a particular topic. For in his mind the elements of covenant, tabernacle, and sacrifices constitute a unity which is self-contained. Over all the instruments of religion are the Covenants (Old and New) which God has made with his people through the ages; under these Covenants, the two tabernacles (the earthly and the heavenly) have been appointed as places for God and man to draw nigh to each other; and it is in these that the sacrifices (animal and Christ's) are offered.

In line with this unity, it should be noted that the present section and the one in verses 11-14 begin in very much the same manner and furnish us to an extent with a repetition of the same ideas. There is, however, a new aspect introduced into the argument in the present section. This concerns the implications for worship and for man's salvation generally which the existence of the heavenly sanctuary brings to light. These may be said to include the following: First, inasmuch as the true sanctuary is in "heaven itself" (vs. 24), our Lord may be said to have appeared "in the presence of God" in a way that was denied to even the high priest as he entered into the inner Holy of Holies of the earthly Tabernacle. This will be seen to have significance for those who follow Jesus into the sanctuary (10:19; see by contrast 9:8). Again, our

Lord's entrance as High Priest into the heavenly sanctuary need
not be performed "repeatedly" (vs. 25). Repetitions of this type,
as the author has already indicated, serve to show the nonvalidity
of the sacrifices thus presented (vss. 8-10). This is because such
sacrifices are associated only with the things of "this creation"
(vs. 11) rather than with those of "heaven itself" (vs. 24). And
they have no more final character than any other events attaching
to the earthly plane. In consequence, Christ, had he been an
earthly high priest, "would have had to suffer repeatedly since the
foundation of the world" (vs. 26). His sacrifice, it is true, was offered on the earthly plane and "at the end of the age," but it had
heavenly associations which were denied to the sacrifices of the
Levitical priests; it was "the sacrifice of himself," that is, of the
eternal Son and "through the eternal Spirit" (vs. 14). This personal, heavenly character of our Lord's sacrifice set it apart from
all others which preceded it. The "now" in verse 24 is intended to
make clear this subtle relation between the historical and the
eternal nature of Christ's sacrifice, a relation which is wholly
unique. The earthly and the heavenly are "once for all" united in
the "now" of Jesus Christ's sacrifice.

Finally, this "once for all" aspect of the work of Christ is asserted in the form of an analogy drawn from common experience.
It is a well-known fact that in the natural order there is a finality
attaching to death. Man, then, can look forward to nothing intervening before the coming of the "judgment" of God (vs. 27). Our
author now sees a similar finality about the work of Christ. His
offering "to bear the sins of many" is just as final as the death of
men on the plane of human affairs. Nor will anything intervene
between that death and his coming "a second time" for the salvation of his people (vs. 28). And here our author expresses his
thought with a quotation ("to bear the sins of many") taken from
Isaiah 53:12 and the description of the work of the Suffering
Servant of the Lord. Although the author employs throughout the
imagery of the high priesthood of Melchizedek, he shares the
common conviction of the Early Church that our Lord in his
work and ministry fulfilled the concept of the Suffering Servant.

The Once-for-All Aspect of the Son's High-Priestly Work
(10:1-18)

The author now sets out to justify what he terms the "once for

all" nature of the sacrifice of Jesus Christ (vs. 10; see 9:26). He
does this first by pointing out that "the law," like the former
Tabernacle, has merely "a shadow of the good things to come,"
that is, the realities to which it points forward (vs. 1; see 8:5).
When he speaks of "the law" he undoubtedly has in mind the Mosaic ceremonial legislation with regard to sacrifice, as the entire argument clearly indicates. The words which he uses ("shadow" for
the legal regulations and "true form" for the sacrifice of Christ)
correspond to the fact that he has called the former Tabernacle
merely "a copy and shadow" (8:5), whereas the heavenly sanctuary into which Christ as High Priest enters is the original "pattern" shown to Moses in the Mount. And he makes the point—only
hinted at previously (9:25-26)—that the yearly sacrifices on the
Day of Atonement offered by the Jewish high priest served as "a
reminder of sin" (vs. 3), creating in the worshiper a "consciousness of sin" (vs. 2), and therefore a conviction that he had not
been cleansed or saved by such legal sacrifices. He concludes this
part of his discussion with the statement of his conviction that "it
is impossible that the blood of bulls and goats should take away
sins" (vs. 4). Essentially this argument amounts to what he has
already said at 9:9-10 and 13—that the animal sacrifices under
the Law only served to maintain the ritual worship in functioning
order.

It is clear from the statement of his case that the author's
major interest in this letter, as we have already had reason to
note (2:11; 9:14), relates to the sanctification or inner cleansing
of the worshiper from a "consciousness of sin" (vs. 2). It is such
inner cleansing that he equates with making perfect (vss. 1 and
14). This is not to say that the writer is not aware of the more objective side of salvation; indeed, he comes close to the Pauline
teaching with regard to justification in several passages (10:38;
11:4, 7).

The author now indicates the "once for all" adequacy of Jesus
Christ's sacrifice, using as a new approach a quotation from
Psalm 40:6-8. This is admittedly neither a "royal" nor "suffering
servant" Psalm. The quotation, however, is relevant to the needs
of the writer at the moment, inasmuch as it affirms the valueless-
ness of the sacrifices prescribed under the Law. In the Hebrew
original the psalmist contrasts such sacrificial offerings with the
fact that, as he says of the Lord, "thou hast given me an open
ear." The Greek translation of this last clause is rendered "a

body hast thou prepared for me." The meaning is doubtless the same, and both Hebrew and Greek have the worshiper declare, "Lo, I have come to do thy will, O God." It is this doing of the divine will upon which Hebrews lays stress (vs. 9).

The author's application of these verses to the Incarnation ("when Christ came into the world," vs. 5) has the general justification which attaches to the employment of another's language to articulate one's own thought. It is to be noted that the New Testament nowhere makes further use of this quotation from the Psalm. It is instructive to note, however, that verse 9 of the Psalm, which our author does not quote, contains the phrase "the glad news of deliverance," which the psalmist says he has announced "in the great congregation." It may be argued that the "glad news" referred to here is the gospel in embryo. In any case, the author of Hebrews fastened on the passage as one qualified to articulate his own thought that over against the many sacrifices of Judaism, which serve only as reminders of their inadequacy to cleanse man's conscience, Jesus Christ's self-offering ("a body hast thou prepared for me" and "I have come to do thy will, O God") is something new in the realm of sacrificial worship. Here is the self-giving of a Person on behalf of persons. It is a giving which functions in the realm of spirit, and accordingly the deduction may be drawn that "we have been sanctified through the offering of the body of Jesus Christ once for all" (vs. 10).

It should be noted that in both the Hebrew and the Greek (whose thought-frames in the New Testament spring from the Hebrew), "body" stands for the entire active person. In consequence, to give one's body is the same as to give one's self, as is intended in the saying at verse 7—"Lo, I have come to do thy will, O God." The teaching of the passage is generally in accord with that of 2:10-18. As there, so here, the identification with mankind on Jesus' part which was accomplished at the Incarnation had in view the final Atonement and the surrender of his body wholly to do the will of God. And once more, as at 9:11-14, the cogency of his argument resides in the spiritual difference observable between the offering of "the blood of bulls and goats" (10:4) and the offering of "the body of Jesus Christ" (10:10).

The third argument which our author at this point presents in favor of the once-for-allness of Christ's sacrifice is found in the different postures of the priests under the two Covenants. The Levitical priests are compelled to stand daily in their service of sacrifice (vs. 11); but, as shown in the quotation from Psalm 110:1 (already employed in several contexts, see 1:3, 13; 8:1), Jesus Christ after making his "single sacrifice for sins" is able to sit down at the right hand of God (vs. 12). This is the act of one who knows that he has accomplished the task he was given to do and that God has accepted his work as final. Scripture, therefore, is justification for the conclusion that "by a single offering he has perfected for all time those who are sanctified" (vs. 14).

Finally, the author again draws upon the passage from Jeremiah 31:33-34 relative to the New Covenant—a Covenant which he assumes his readers will now agree to be the one under which our Lord's high priesthood may be said to function—as proof that in the work of Christ there is no longer a remembrance of sins, and that in consequence these have received forgiveness (vss. 17-18). There is, therefore, as he remarks, "no longer any offering for sin" required.

The argument of this passage once again suggests the possibility that Hebrews has in mind the teachings of the Qumran sect. This group had rejected the sacrifices of the Temple and held that "the offering of the lips"—presumably of prayer and praise—was more acceptable in the sight of God than all offerings and sacrifices. Hebrews also knows of the sacrifice which prayer entails, and it teaches a doctrine of a High Priest who "always lives to make intercession" for his people (7:25). But in the present passage the concern is to point out that intercession is an inadequate substitute for sacrifice, if man's sins are to be forgiven. Forgiveness and purification require rather the substitution of human sacrifice for animal sacrifice, of a High Priest who offers himself for man's sin in place of priests appointed to make offerings which do not intimately touch the human spirit.

THE RESPONSE REQUIRED OF SONS TO THE HIGH-PRIESTLY WORK OF THE SON

Hebrews 10:19—13:17

Summary Statement (10:19-31)

We come now to the last major section of the letter. There is a certain co-ordination between this section and the second major

division beginning at 3:1 and running through 4:16. There the
author was dealing with the gospel call to the sons to become
"God's house." That call was issued in view of the general testimony which had been given to the redemptive power and lordship of God's Son. In the meantime the author has sketched out
the nature of the Son's high priesthood and the efficacy of his
high-priestly work. Appropriately, therefore, he issues the gospel
call again and this time on the foundation laid in the intervening
sections from 5:1—10:18.

It is not surprising, then, to notice that the call is issued in almost identical language with that at 4:14-16. The approximation
of the language is far closer in the Greek than in the English
translation. Note the similarities between 4:14 and 10:19-21 and
between 4:16 and 10:22. Other similarities in thought if not in
word are found in the two passages; for example, at 4:15 the
author stresses Jesus' ability to sympathize with our weaknesses
in view of his own temptations, while at 10:20 reference is made
to the "way . . . through his flesh," that is, to the Incarnation as
the method adopted to prepare man's approach to God.

It is clear that the author's argument relative to the Son's high-
priestly work in the fourth major section of the letter (8:1—
10:18) has carried him far beyond the analogy previously drawn
between Christ as High Priest and Melchizedek (5:1—7:28).
Though in their eternal character a real similarity is seen between
the two priesthoods, Melchizedek never went so far as to offer
himself as a living sacrifice to God on behalf of man. It is only
"by the blood of Jesus" (vs. 19) that we may have "confidence to
enter the sanctuary" and so enjoy eternal fellowship with God.
Jesus' "blood" is specified as the means of access to God, as has
already been done at 9:12 and 14. But, as we have already seen,
such mention is made there in deference to the comparison to the
blood of "goats and calves" offered by the high priest on the Day
of Atonement, and essentially the reference is to Christ's offering of "himself" (9:14) or of his "body" (10:5-10).

The method of salvation is now described as "the new and living way which he opened for us through the curtain, that is,
through his flesh" (vs. 20). The reference is undoubtedly to the
method chosen by our Lord to redeem man, which was one of incarnation followed by atonement and resurrection. The adjective
"new" applied to this way actually means "fresh" as opposed to
decomposed and may be taken as the equivalent of "living." Prob-

ably verse 20 should read: "By the new and living way of his flesh
which he opened for us through the curtain," rather than as in the
Revised Standard Version. Interpreters differ on whether "flesh"
here is to be taken with "way" or with "curtain." But the "curtain" which our author has in mind is that separating the Holy
Place from the Holy of Holies and designed to indicate that
"the way into the sanctuary is not yet opened as long as the outer
tent is still standing" (9:8). It is impossible that, in the mind of
any Christian writer of the first century, Jesus' flesh should typify
that curtain or vice versa. There is no evidence in the New Testament that Jesus' flesh was thought of as an obscuring medium or
one intended to hide his divinity. On the contrary, the only passage which makes reference to a veil or curtain obscuring God's
glory from man is II Corinthians 3:7-18. And there it is quite
clear that the veil is man's blindness which makes it impossible
for him to behold God's truth and that "only through Christ is it
taken away" (II Cor. 3:14). Indeed, in the present verse the
preposition "through" before the words "his flesh" is not found
in the Greek, and if the author's intention had been that we should
read "through the curtain of his flesh," obviously the phrase "that
is" would not have been required. It is through "the living way of
his flesh"—that is, through the Incarnation and the resulting
Atonement and Resurrection—that Jesus leads onward "through
the curtain" which separates man from God.

There is a striking similarity between our author's argument at
this point and that of Paul in I Corinthians 5:7-8 relative to the
nature of the Christian life. Paul there compares the Christian
life to a continuous Passover festival from which "the leaven of
malice and evil" has been removed so that Christians may live
their lives upon "the unleavened bread of sincerity and truth."
Similarly, Hebrews conceives of the Christian way of life as a
continuous Day of Atonement.

In the life of service three things particularly are of importance
and should be practiced by every son of God. First, there is the
coming to God "in full assurance of faith" (vs. 22). Such assurance is based upon the cleansing "from an evil conscience" which,
as the author has already indicated, is possible only through the
offering of Christ (9:14), that is, through the action of one person for another, the personal factor of faith or trust being the
uniting spark between the two. The reference to "our bodies
washed with pure water" is without doubt a reference to baptism,

which the Early Church considered the mark of saving witness (see Rom. 6:1-8), and to which the author has already referred (6:2). Second, as before, he suggests that we must "hold fast the confession of our hope without wavering" (vs. 23; see 3:6, 14; 6:11). This "hope," as we have already seen, is by no means a weak one. Rather, it is as certain as anything may be in the spiritual realm. It is the "sure and steadfast anchor of the soul" which Jesus has affixed to the mercy seat within the curtain (6:19-20). Moreover, as our author now adds, the certainty of its fulfillment is based upon the promise of God who is above all else "faithful." Third, we are to "meet together" in corporate endeavor to fulfill the demands of worship on this continuous Day of Atonement. And our fellowship is to be one of stimulus "to love and good works" (vs. 24). Of this more will be said in succeeding sections.

Reference has previously been made to the fact that Christians are living in the eschatological time, or, as our author says, in "these last days" (1:2). Such was the common belief of the early Christian Church which produced the New Testament Scriptures (see Mark 1:15; Phil. 4:5; James 5:8-9). The end of this eschatological period would be the Day of Judgment or, to employ Amos' phrase, "the day of the LORD" (Amos 5:18). There can be no doubt that it is this great Day which the author has in mind in verse 25, as the succeeding verses clearly indicate. This is the Day of Judgment for all men, Christians and pagans alike, and the author suggests that the Christian life should be lived in constant awareness of the demands of him who is the Judge of all men.

Verses 26 to 31 contain the author's reason for suggesting that the Day of Judgment should stand for us as an incentive to right living. Essentially the argument is based upon his conception of the once-for-allness involved in every event in the series of righteous acts which together constitute God's relation to his world and particularly to men. He has already asserted the once-for-all character of the self-sacrifice of Jesus Christ as man's High Priest (7:27; 9:12). Moreover, he has declared that this once-for-allness guarantees that "there is no longer any offering for sin" (vs. 18). The present passage, therefore, is a reminder that if this one sacrifice is spurned, "there no longer remains a sacrifice for sins" (vs. 26). And, indeed, what further consideration may Christians who have spurned "the truth" expect? For to deny the once-for-allness of the unique sacrifice of Jesus Christ is essentially to deny the Christian faith. This is the final apostasy.

Such persons have nothing save "a fearful prospect of judgment" to which they may look forward (vs. 27). Those who deny the validity of Christ's sacrifice and so of the Christian faith have placed themselves alongside pagans, of whom our author has already written, "it is appointed for men to die once, and after that comes judgment" (9:27). And as in other places our author has adopted the argument from the less to the greater (see 9:13-14), in comparing the older revelation with the new, so here he argues for a "much worse punishment" for Christians who have denied the light they received in Jesus Christ than for those who have merely "violated the law of Moses" (vss. 28-29).

Hebrews' analysis of this type of apostasy (vs. 29) includes three things: (1) spurning the Son of God and his sacrifice for man; (2) holding that "the blood of the covenant" is a common thing incapable of sanctifying, that is, of rendering the worshiper fit to approach God in fellowship; and (3) arrogantly spurning the offices of the gracious Spirit who has been present in the community (2:4; 6:4; 9:8) and in the work of Jesus Christ himself (9:14). The author assures his readers that the promises of judgment proclaimed by the Lord to his people are as certain as the promises of grace (compare 4:1-10 and Deut. 32:35-36; Ps. 135: 14). His argument here is the same as that running through the prophetic writings of the Old Testament and Jesus' teachings (see, for example, Amos 3:2). Jesus summarizes this point of view in his words, "Every one to whom much is given, of him will much be required; and of him to whom men commit much they will demand the more" (Luke 12:48b). The argument then comes necessarily to the conclusion that God is as surely "the living God" to punish as "the living God" to bless and to save (vs. 31; see 3:12; 9:14).

Examples of Faith (Hope) (10:32—11:40)

The Readers (10:32-39)

Following the above section in which response to the gospel call is briefly developed along the lines of faith, hope, and love (the trilogy made famous by Paul in I Corinthians 13), stress is now laid upon "faith" as the expression of the sons' response required in the present condition of the readers. Three things stand out in this passage as peculiarly noteworthy: first, the psychological value attaching to commendation of previous worthy action on the part of people with whom one is counseling; second, the historical detail involved in the presentation of the example; and third, the encouragement to be derived from the author's eschatological views.

It is clear from the passage that shortly after the readers had been baptized ("enlightened," that is, awakened to spiritual apprehension by the Holy Spirit; see 6:4; Eph. 1:18), they had been subjected to persecution involving "hard struggle with sufferings," public abuse, the imprisonment of some, the "plundering" of "property," and the courageous sharing of sufferings generally among the Christian community (vss. 32-34). There is considerable difference of opinion among New Testament interpreters as to the occasion referred to in this description (see Introduction). The persecution was apparently not as violent as those under the Roman emperors, when Christians were persecuted for the sacred name of Christ and wholesale slaughter was practiced in many cases. There is here no suggestion that any lost their lives. The statement at 12:4, "you have not yet resisted to the point of shedding your blood," probably refers to the entire Christian experience of the readers. It may be, therefore, that this persecution is the one experienced by the Hellenistic-Jewish branch of the Church in the very early days in Jerusalem and the nearby vicinity (Acts 8:1-3). In any case, the author appeals to the readers' conviction that they have "a better possession and an abiding one" (vs. 34). It is this "confidence" to which he had already referred in 3:14, a confidence leading to our "share in Christ" or, as here, "a great reward" (vs. 35). As throughout the letter, the stress is upon the "need of endurance" that his readers may "inherit the promises" (6:12). It is this endurance which lies within "the will of God" (vs. 36).

With a view to lightening the load to be placed upon his readers, the author now quotes from Habakkuk 2:3-4 to the effect that the endurance required is for only "a little while." The promised coming of Jesus Christ "a second time" (see 9:28) as High Priest is seen in the perspective of God's eternal purpose to save mankind. Though no temporal span of an exact nature may be indicated nor a chronological scheme worked out, nonetheless, for any generation of Christians, endurance is for but "a little while." In the meantime, God's righteous people must "live by faith"—not by sight but by perseverance in the Christian faith. And, as before at 6:9-12 so now, the readers are assured that they are "not of those who shrink back and are destroyed, but of those who have faith and keep their souls" (vs. 39). The psychological value of this sort of argument is obvious, as well as Christian.

Old Testament Worthies (11:1-40)

The second example of faith as response to the gospel call is derived from the experience of the Old Testament worthies referred to by name or inference in the present chapter. Before enumerating the examples which he has chosen, the author first calls the attention of his readers to the remarkable power of faith as response to God's word and the fact that it wins "divine approval" (vss. 1-3).

This would seem to be the proper point in the study of this letter to summarize Hebrews' teaching on the subject of faith. Examination of the various passages in which the term is used reveals the fact that for the author: (1) faith is the one response which God expects of those who have heard the gospel call (4:2); (2) fundamentally such faith depends upon God (6:1-3), and so may be defined as personal attachment or trust; (3) such trust results primarily in man's receiving "the promises" of God to his people (6:12; 11:13, 39-40); (4) it stimulates "assurance" of one's acceptance among God's people at the throne of grace (10:22) and of being numbered among the saved (10:39); (5) it is the means whereby man perceives and accepts the divine philosophy of history (11:3); (6) it has implications for the Christian life, providing God's people with the courage requisite to living victoriously in a sinful world (11:6-7, 33-38); (7) it is the spiritual bond between Jesus, "the pioneer and perfecter of our faith," and his people (12:2); (8) and accordingly it makes its possessor "an heir of the righteousness which comes by faith" only, which means God's final approval of his people and his acceptance of them (11:6-7; 13:7).

In the present chapter the author makes it his object to show that faith exhibits the miraculous power of dissolving the time-space framework in which men live their lives. This is its primary function, and it accomplishes this for every man in the context in which he lives. No matter what his temporal and spatial limitations be, faith sets him in a large place from which he can see the distant scene from the perspective of God. The chapter opens with a description of how faith operates along the lines just suggested and thereafter follows a series of illustrations of the point.

"Faith," says our author, is related to "things hoped for," that is, those things which are beyond the boundaries set by the time dimension of man's life. Similarly, it is related to "things not seen," that is, things beyond the space boundary set by the human eye (vs. 1). Two Greek words in the verse indicate what faith is capable of doing to these temporal and spatial boundaries. The first word, translated "assurance," relates to the underlying structure or content of anything which makes it what it is. However, the term is used eventually in many ways, and its context in this chapter would suggest that our writer may have in mind something like its use as "a title deed." A title deed is that which is guaranteed to give substance to a piece of property which one has purchased. And the context of the present chapter, indeed that of the entire essay, indicates that for the writer faith is "a title deed" which gives substance to the things beyond the barrier set by the time dimension of the framework of our lives. Similarly, the second term is one used in the common parlance of the day for "a lawyer's brief" as well as for the "conviction" established by such a brief in the mind of the judge(s). Faith, then, is the lawyer's brief which "convicts" us of God's verities which lie beyond the spatial barrier of our lives. Little wonder that those who employ such faith receive the "divine approval" (vs. 2), for in doing so they are adding a divine dimension to their lives; they are set in a large place from which they may view life and the world according to the divine perspective.

Before giving examples from among the Old Testament worthies who had this faith, the author suggests that it is by "faith" that men come to understand history. Pagan peoples see no need for a doctrine which separates the Creator from the created. But the God of history, of the Hebrew prophets, and of the Christian faith is a God of every part of history, including its beginning and its end. He started the series of events which constitute history, he is the Providence who never deserts it, and he will conclude it in his own good time. This view of God and the world is one accepted "by faith." That "the world was created by the word of God" (vs. 3) is the view stressed both in Genesis 1 and in John 1 (see also Rom. 1:20). Already, therefore, our author has in a quite subtle fashion indicated that his readers have "by faith" been removed from the time-space framework of their lives. With its long arm they have, as it were, reached out to the very beginning of time and history and brought even the events of the creation epoch within the sphere of their own interests, discerning their relevance for themselves.

The three examples of men of faith in the period before Abraham are particularly apt (Abel, Enoch, and Noah). Abel is chosen because it is recorded of him that he is the first to bring an offering of sheep (in later years so largely used in the Old Testament sacrificial system with which Hebrews has been dealing), and Genesis 4:4 asserts that "the LORD had regard for Abel and his offering." Though the account of this incident does not say so, it may well be argued that it is "by faith" (vs. 4) that Abel makes his offering to God. At any rate, no Jew could deny that Abel's offering was a more acceptable one than that of Cain, as the later Levitical sacrifices appeared to substantiate. The common Semitic practice of sacrifice and belief in its general acceptance in the eyes of God formed the background for the argument.

The argument with reference to Hebrews' second example (that of Enoch) is based on Genesis 5:21-24. Of Enoch it was said that he "walked with God." This is interpreted in Hebrews to mean that he "was attested as having pleased God" (vs. 5). From the Christian standpoint it is evident that "without faith it is impossible to please him" (vs. 6), from which it may be deduced that Enoch had faith in God. The argument that those who, like Enoch, "would draw near to God" should as a minimum "believe that he exists" (vs. 6) is perhaps not entirely happy in its expression. For as James remarks, "Even the demons believe" in the oneness of God (James 2:19). It must be remembered, however, that the author of Hebrews is consciously dealing with a very rudimentary type of faith. It is pre-Abrahamic faith, or, if one prefer, the type of faith shown by a man quite outside the boundaries of the Chosen People of God. No doubt these early examples are chosen deliberately to exhibit the *breadth* of the Christian faith; for its *depth* and *height,* however, we must look elsewhere.

Of the three examples chosen from beyond the pale of the "people of God" (11:25), the example of Noah is by far the clearest. Genesis 6:13-22 and, indeed, the entire account regarding Noah give evidence of a special call which Noah received and of special revelation made to him regarding God's will. Accordingly, in the early Christian Church much was made of the example of Noah as "a herald of righteousness" in a sinful world (II Peter 2:5). In one account of the eschatological discourse of our Lord, Noah figures as an example of the man of God who, by reason of his faith, is ready for "the coming of the Son of man" at the end of history (Matt. 24:37-39; Luke 17:26-27). In I Peter 3:18-20, Noah is made to serve as the typical person who through baptism has come within "the ark" and thus may be said to be "saved through water." Christian art of the period of the catacombs and persecutions makes much of this example of Noah, and of the ark, in representing the Church itself.

Accordingly, Noah could be held up as an example of one who by faith had become aware of "events as yet unseen" and who might be said, therefore, to have burst the temporal and spatial boundaries and come to view the events of history as God sees them. In so doing he clearly "condemned the world," its small perspective, its little framework of reference. One might well be assured, therefore, that Noah had become "an heir of the righteousness which comes by faith" (vs. 7).

Perhaps we should be interpreting the writer's mind with accuracy if we were to conclude that in Noah, Abel, and Enoch he has chosen the three examples outside the pale of revealed religion in the pre-Abrahamic days who best exemplify the fact of God's redeeming grace and his earnest wish to save all those who sincerely turn to him in faith. It is not, however, until we come to Abraham, "the father of the faithful," that a number of the distinctively Christian words with which we have become familiar in the letter are used. These include the ideas of the gospel "call" (5:4; 9:15), "obedience" and its opposite (3:18; 5:9), "inheritance" (6:12; 9:15), "promise" (4:1; 6:12; 7:6; 8:6; 9:15; 10:23, 36), and even the thought involved in the phrase "to go out" or "exodus" (3:16; 13:13).

All this means that for the author, as well as for the Jewish people before him, Abraham occupied a special position of importance in the scheme of the redemption of God's people. With Abraham it may be said that special revelation began. Moreover, it began with a "call" to go out from among the people of the world with a view to occupying a distinctive position in God's economy of redemption. In both the Old and the New Testaments a "call" is by no means an abstraction. It does not appear out of the void or without an author. Rather, the "call" of Scripture always emanates directly from God. It is significant, too, that to Abraham as representative of the about-to-be-formed "people of God" the call came "to go out to a place which he was to receive as an inheritance" (vs. 8). That is to say, Abraham was called out of the context (the time-space framework) in which his life had thus far been lived. His life was now to know new horizons, to start anew in a place of new perspectives. He was to find "in the land of promise" a point of vantage from which to view life as God views it.

The limitless horizons of this place are indicated by the words, "he went out, not knowing where he was to go." Moreover, that the place specified is by no means a final fulfillment of the promise of "an inheritance" is stressed. Abraham was not led, nor were his descendants, to imagine that the "land of promise" was a total fulfillment of the promises of God. Rather he looked upon that land as a "foreign land" in which he and his descendants merely "sojourned" (vs. 9). The transitory nature of their abode is shown also in the fact that they were continually "living in tents." God had directed their eyes to a more permanent abode, in fact, "to the city which has foundations, whose builder and maker is God" (vs. 10). The permanence of city life, with its "foundations," as over against a casual existence "in tents," lends itself admirably to the contrast which the author wishes to make between the eternal and the transitory (vs. 16).

The use of the concept of a city to describe the permanent character of the inheritance of God's people is by no means limited to Hebrews. It is a striking characteristic, for example, of the Revelation to John (Rev. 3:12; 11:2; 20:9; 21:2). The idea no doubt derives originally from the prophetic thought that "the LORD of hosts will reign on Mount Zion and in Jerusalem" (Isa. 24:23; 27:13; Micah 4:7). The idea that the people of God are merely "strangers and exiles on the earth" (vs. 13), and accordingly are "seeking a homeland" in the eternal order (vs. 14), is also not new with Hebrews. The thought derives from Genesis 23:4 so far as Abraham is concerned, and it is related in general to God's people elsewhere in the Old Testament (Ezek. 20:38). Paul makes use of the idea in Philippians 3:20 with the remark that "our commonwealth is in heaven," an expression which suggests that Christians in the world are, so to speak, colonists abroad from their homeland!

Throughout the passage, in accordance with the thought expressed in verses 1 and 2, faith is treated as the instrument by means of which God's people view the transitory world and all it contains in true perspective. The phrase "by faith" occurs again and again like a refrain. For it is only "by faith" that God's people are enabled to assess the transitory and the eternal at their proper values. There is a very real sense in which in this life they have not "received what was promised, but having seen and greeted it from afar" they live their lives in the perspective of God (vs. 13).

Not alone Abraham, but his wife Sarah as well (vs. 11), his son Isaac, his grandsons Jacob and Esau, and his great-grandson Joseph (vss. 17-22) are said to have possessed the requisite faith. Sarah's faith is particularly significant because she had already, along with Abraham, passed the age when children are expected in the home (vss. 11-12; see Gen. 17:19; 18:11-14). Abraham was already "as good as dead." God's faithfulness in fulfilling his promises (vs. 11), therefore, was shown provisionally in the fact that from this old couple were born "descendants as many as the stars of heaven." Hebrews specifically states, as we have observed, that this is not the final fulfillment of God's promise to his people (vs. 13). But the fact is not to be ignored that it does represent a partial fulfillment—an "earnest" of the final one toward which God's people may look forward. It is a parable, so to speak, of life from the dead, which is of the very essence of the salvation which God holds out for man. And it is not unlike the gift of the Holy Spirit, which, as Paul observes, is "the guarantee of our inheritance until we acquire possession of it" (Eph. 1:14).

The incident involving Abraham's testing when he was "ready to offer up his only son" Isaac (vs. 17) carries essentially the same thought as that involved in Isaac's birth. In both cases Abraham "considered that God was able to raise men even from the dead," from which, as our author suggests, "figuratively speaking, he did receive him back" (vss. 17-19). For, however one is to understand the story in its original form at Genesis 22:1-10, in Hebrews it is seen in the light of the promise which God had made to Abraham—"Through Isaac shall your descendants be named." This promise Abraham at all times was prepared to believe, whatever the transitory evidence of earthly existence might appear to suggest to the contrary.

In the case of Abraham's descendants, the incidents chosen for comment are those concerned with the end of the life of each when he "blessed" his descendants, and the author's point has to do with the faith thereby exhibited (vss. 20-22). The stress here, as previously throughout the chapter, is upon a faith which looks beyond the immediate horizons to the fulfillment of God's promises to his people. And it should be observed that in laying stress upon this faith the author is true to the spirit of the Old Testament at the points involved (Gen. 27:27-40; 48:21; 50:24-25; Exod. 13:19). In the case of Joseph, his faith leaps forward to the Exodus and he gives "directions concerning his burial" in the land of promise. This mention of "the exodus" from Egypt naturally leads on to the next character with which our author wishes to deal, namely, the lawgiver Moses.

Abraham and Moses are the two focal points of the Old Testament revelation. The Christian Church, arising as it did out of the context of Judaism, inherited the sense of the prominence of these two Old Testament worthies. (For the importance of Moses see Mark 9:4-5; John 3:14; Acts 3:22; Revelation 15:3.)

There was, however, from the beginning this marked difference between Judaism and the Christian faith with reference to the parts played by Abraham and Moses. For Pharisaism, the dominant school of thought in the Judaism of the first century, Moses played the more prominent part, and his ministry served as a norm by which to gauge all of the revelation under the Old Covenant, including that made to Abraham. Accordingly, Abraham was interpreted in the light of the revelation which Judaism held to have come through Moses. He was said, for example, to have fulfilled the Law in its entirety before Moses appeared on the scene. His perfection, or salvation, was said to have occurred only after his circumcision and because of it. In the Early Church, however, the roles of these two were reversed. Abraham became the standard, so that the Law given to Moses was to be understood in the light of the revelation which came to Abraham. Paul spoke of this revelation as the "gospel" (Gal. 3:8) and averred that the Law, which came 430 years afterward, could not annul the Covenant previously ratified by God with Abraham (Gal. 3:17); while in opposition to the viewpoint of Pharisaism cited above, he argued that "faith was reckoned to Abraham as righteousness . . . before he was circumcised" (Rom. 4:9-10).

It need not surprise us, then, that Hebrews at this point is not concerned about the Law which was promulgated through Moses but rather about his "faith." Moreover, it was faith and the courage born of it which the author sees exemplified in the parents of Moses (vs. 23), by the people who followed Moses' leadership at the Exodus, by the army of Israel in the conquest of Canaan as at Jericho (vss. 29-30), and by Rahab the harlot who gave assistance to the two spies sent in to spy out the land (vs. 31).

It is noteworthy that in his account of Moses' "choosing rather to share ill-treatment with the people of God than to enjoy the fleeting pleasures of sin" (vs. 25), our author suggests that he was prepared to suffer "for the Christ" (vs. 26). The New Testament writers in general look back and see all previous events in the redemptive history of the people of God in the light of Christ. Accordingly, it is the author's viewpoint that Moses' sufferings can be thought of as eventually for Christ's sake, because Moses as the leader of God's people was in the divine succession of events experienced by that people, a succession whose culminating event was to be Christ.

This interpretation runs parallel, then, with the author's view of Abraham. For on the one hand he can speak of him as one who, "having patiently endured, obtained the promise" (6:15), and on the other as numbered among all those who "though well attested by their faith, did not receive what was promised" (11:39). That is to say, Hebrews sees both a proximate and a remote fulfillment of God's promises to his people at all times. And to this phenomenon neither Abraham nor Moses is an exception. Abraham did receive the promise in the sense that "he sojourned in the land of promise" (vs. 9); but in a larger sense he was numbered among all those who "died in faith, not having received what was promised, but having seen it and greeted it from afar" (vs. 13). In like manner for the author, Moses was rewarded through a long period of years with the leadership of God's people, but in a real sense the remote possession was never obtained by him; rather, "he endured as seeing him who is invisible" (vs. 27).

And now the author concludes his argument with a summary statement, because, as he suggests, "time would fail" him to give a complete account of all the Old Testament worthies who exemplified the response of faith which God desires of man (vs. 32). His summary is a very comprehensive one. Following the conquest of Canaan, which is suggested by his choice of Rahab (vs. 31), he begins with the judges—Gideon, Barak, Samson, Jephthah (vs. 32)—and then proceeds to David as God's choice for setting up the theocracy in Israel, and comprehends the entire Hebrew prophetic movement in the words "Samuel and the prophets" (vs. 32). Thereafter, in verses 33-38, he summarizes the experiences of the faithful throughout the period of the remaining Old Testament and Intertestament literature.

Most, if not all, of the references can be identified, and they introduce us to a wide range of characters whose lives exemplified the faith with which the author is dealing. Thus, of those "who through faith conquered kingdoms" he may very well have in mind men like Joshua and David. Those who "enforced justice" would very properly include the judges and kings like David and Solomon. Daniel is obviously one who "stopped the mouths of lions" (Dan. 6:21-23). Perhaps he and his associates in Babylon are also in mind as those who "quenched raging fire" (Dan. 3: 23-25). According to Isaiah, Hezekiah by the faith shown in his prayer was the means of putting Sennacherib and his armies to flight (II Kings 19:20-37). The widow of Zarephath and the Shunammite woman are examples of the women who "received their dead by resurrection" (I Kings 17:8-24; II Kings 4:18-37). A number of the prophets were "tortured" (see Matt. 5:11-12), notably Jeremiah (Jer., chs. 20, 37-38). Zechariah, the son of Jehoiada, was stoned (II Chron. 24:21). According to an apocryphal book, Isaiah the prophet was among those who were "sawn in two" (Ascension of Isaiah 5:11-14). Verses 35b-38, indeed, sound very much like a summary of the treatment which Israel and the pagan world gave to the Hebrew prophets. Elijah, for example, in the treatment accorded to him by King Ahab of Israel may very well be in the writer's mind as one who went "wandering over deserts and mountains, and in dens and caves of the earth" (I Kings, chs. 18-19).

In the concluding paragraph (vss. 39-40), the author summarizes in a brief statement the point which the entire chapter is intended to illustrate. This is twofold: first, that the reward of faith is never immediately realized. For none of these Old Testament saints received the fulfillment of the promise in its final form. Had it been otherwise, then faith would no longer be faith. For, as the author indicated in the opening paragraph of the chapter, faith places one outside the boundaries of time and space whence one may view the distant scene, but while one lives within those boundaries only proximate realization of the promises of God may ever be experienced. Second, faith always has in view, as does the promise itself, that great company of the faithful whose arrival on the plane of history must precede the fulfillment of the promises. This is the true "communion of the saints"—a fellowship, not alone among those existing at any moment upon the earth, but extending horizontally throughout time, an ever-widening circle of men and women responding by faith to the promises of God.

Exhortation to Endurance as Sons (12:1-29)

The Endurance of the Pioneer and Perfecter of Our Faith (12:1-2)

Hebrews now turns more particularly to the response required of its readers to the high-priestly work of the Son of God. The author thinks of the ancient heroes of faith as a great "cloud of witnesses" surrounding the contemporary generation of the Christian community. His words suggest that he has in mind the spectators in an amphitheater viewing the athletic games of the day, or those who have already run their part of the race. It is to be noted, however, that he does not ask his readers to keep their attention riveted upon this "cloud of witnesses." In point of fact, any athlete who did that would never win the race. The athlete keeps his attention upon the goal post or, alternatively, upon the runner who is at the head of the race. Similarly, the readers are exhorted to continue "looking to Jesus the pioneer and perfecter of our faith." For it is clear that it is Jesus who sets the pace and determines the goal of the Christian race.

The worst impediment in the Christian race is the "sin which clings so closely" to every runner. The King James Version at this point translated, "the sin which doth so easily beset us," and as a result there is a popular conception among Christians that each person has a different "besetting sin." But this is certainly not the meaning of the author. There is nothing in the Greek to suggest a particularly besetting sin attaching to one Christian rather than another. The author is exhorting his readers to lay aside "every weight" deriving from background, experience, education, and contemporary culture, as well as the "sin" common to all mankind, in order that they may run without hindrance the race of the Christian life.

As has been said previously in more ways than one, "perseverance" is required in order that the race may be brought to a successful conclusion (see 3:6, 14; 10:36). The Christian is not asked to run in a spectacular fashion, putting on now and again a spurt of speed with a view to making an impression upon spectators. It is rather a sort of dogged stick-to-it-iveness to which the author exhorts his readers. In so doing he is in line with other New Testament writers, notably with Paul (Rom. 2:7; 5:3; 8:25; II Cor. 6:4; Col. 1:11), James (1:3-4), II Peter (1:6), and Revelation (1:9; 2:2; 3:10). This is not an exhaustive list, but it is sufficient to show that the New Testament writers considered "perseverance" ("endurance," "steadfastness," "patience") to be one of the primary "fruits of the Spirit" observable in the Christian life. And inasmuch as such endurance relates to every expression of the Christian faith, it would scarcely be too much to say that it is the all-inclusive fruitage of the Christian experience.

The description which Hebrews gives of Jesus in this passage as "the pioneer and perfecter of our faith" is a notable one. Nowhere else in the New Testament is the term "perfecter" employed with regard to our Lord, and only the Book of Acts also speaks of him as "pioneer." In Acts 3:15 the Greek word is translated "Author" ("of life"), and the context suggests that Luke is impressed with the strange paradox that he who is "the Author of life" has himself been "killed" by unruly and ungodly men. At Acts 5:31, however, the same word is translated "Leader," and there it is combined with the term "Savior."

The expression "Leader and Savior" rather closely approximates that in the present passage. And it is notable that in 2:10 the author combines all three ideas of leadership, salvation, and perfection in one phrase relating to Jesus ("the pioneer of their salvation perfect through suffering"). Certainly, in the present imagery of the race course, "pioneer" is to be taken in the sense of "leader" of the race, that is, of the runner who is far ahead in the Christian way of life. It is toward such a one that the other runners in the Christian way may look for guidance, for leadership, for encouragement, and above all as the goal to be reached. In Ephesians 4:13 Paul expressed the same idea, but under an entirely different figure, in the words, "until we all attain . . . to mature manhood, to the measure of the stature of the fullness of Christ."

This is not to say that as "pioneer and perfecter" of our faith Jesus is merely another runner in the Christian race. To be the leader, the one who sets out the course, is to be far above all others who come after and who follow his pattern. Of no other than the Leader of the faith may it be said that he has "endured the cross, despising the shame, and is seated at the right hand of the throne of God." Strangely enough, nowhere else does the author speak of either "the cross" or "the shame" of our Lord, but both *ideas* have constantly been before us.

Finally, in this passage "the race that is set before us" is paralleled with "the joy that was set before him." The expressions are exactly parallel in the Greek construction as in the English, and this can scarcely be without intention on the author's part. The race stretches out before us even as the joy stretched out before Jesus as he looked to the goal which his Father had set before him in his human life (see 2:9). Probably the meaning, therefore, is that just as he "endured," so should we, both he and we having in mind at all times the high goal set before us by the Father.

The Place of Discipline in Christian Growth (12:3-11)

It is in the context of the idea of Jesus' sufferings that a main theme of the letter is again taken up. The same theme appears in 2:5-18. There the point is made that it is fitting that God, "in bringing many sons to glory, should make the pioneer of their salvation perfect through suffering" (2:10). In the present passage the theme of sonship is elaborated in the same context of suffering (vs. 2). Jesus, whom the "sons" are to emulate, has "endured the cross, despising the shame." It is appropriate in such a context for the author to remind his readers that they "have not yet resisted to the point of shedding . . . blood" (vs. 4). Jesus has endured great "hostility against himself," no doubt of the type which the readers of the letter are now facing (vs. 3).

Obviously, neither the shame of the Cross in Jesus' case nor the hostility now being directed against the readers is the direct work of God. Rather, it is clearly the work of "sinners" (vs. 3) in the case of Jesus; and it is the "sin" of the race against which the readers have to "struggle" (vs. 4). Ultimately the sin in both cases is that of man in his rebellion against God, his Anointed One, and God's people.

And yet, viewed in the perspective of God's redemptive purpose relative to man, both Jesus' sufferings as the Son and those of the "sons" (vss. 5-11) must be thought of as somehow within the divine will and purpose. The author has already expressed the idea that God was behind the suffering of Jesus with a view to making "the pioneer of their salvation perfect" (2:10; see 2:17-18 and 5:8-10). In like manner, it is now to be observed that the "sons" are being asked to endure the "discipline" which will eventuate in their maturing. For such discipline in the end "yields the peaceful fruit of righteousness to those who have been trained by it" (vs. 11).

It is significant that both in the present passage (see vs. 4), and at 10:32-39, wherein the author refers to the persecutions suf-

fered and about to be suffered by his readers, he makes it clear
that none of them has as yet died for the faith. It is difficult, if
not impossible, to believe that either of these persecutions, therefore, has reference to that suffered by the church at Rome under
Nero, when, as Tacitus remarks, burning Christians lit up the
gardens of that emperor.

It is perhaps also not without significance that Hebrews calls
upon the Wisdom Literature (Prov. 3:11-12) to substantiate his
point with regard to God's disciplining of the "sons." This passage is also quoted in Revelation 3:19 in connection with the
chastisement about to be meted out to the church at Laodicea. The
Wisdom Literature was particularly popular among the Hellenistic
Jews from whom we believe the author and his readers to have
emerged.

The central point of the passage is contained in verses 10 and
11—discipline of his "sons" on God's part leads to their sharing
"his holiness" (vs. 10) or to "the peaceful fruit of righteousness"
(vs. 11). As we have already observed, it was natural for our
author, with his stress upon the high-priestly activity of our Lord,
to view salvation in terms of sanctification or of the consecration
of his people for the worship of God (see 2-11; 9:13-14; 10:10,
14, 29). The priestly writer in Leviticus 19:2, in much the same
spirit, had reported God as saying, "You shall be holy; for I the
LORD your God am holy.' In view of his present discussion of the
merits of discipline, it needs no proof that the author of Hebrews,
too, is thinking of the "sons" sharing the moral "holiness" which
is God's. And we may conclude also, in view of the juxtaposition
of verses 10 and 11, that the term "righteousness" is to be understood here as virtually a synonym for "holiness."

The Need of Direction in the Christian Life (12:12-17)

The sons are not to suppose that their share in the matter of
acquiring salvation is a merely passive one. The author turns again
to Proverbs 4:26 (in the Greek version) with a view to suggesting
that the sons are to make straight paths for their feet (vs. 13).
However, he now joins to this quotation another (vs. 12) from
Isaiah 35:3, taken from a chapter devoted by the prophet to
describing the glories of the restored land to which a repentant
Israel should return, over a "highway" which the prophet calls
"the Holy Way" (35:8). It would be only "the ransomed of the
LORD" who would in this way return to Zion (35:10). These ran-

somed are variously described by Isaiah as "the blind," "the deaf," "the lame man," and "the dumb" (35:5-6), and among them are not included "the unclean" and "fools" (35:8-9). That the direction of the Christian way of which Hebrews is speaking leads, like Isaiah's "Holy Way," up to Zion is the theme of the next section (vss. 18-24).

In the meantime, those traveling by the Holy Way are to "strive for peace with all men, and for the holiness without which no one will see the Lord" (vs. 14). The idea that peace between God and man and between man and his neighbor is an accompaniment of salvation is a commonplace in Hebrew prophetic thought (Ps. 85:10; Isa. 57:19). The reference to "holiness" recalls what has been said above in verse 10. But it is likely that the background of the thought here is Psalm 24:4, where the psalmist declares that only those who have "clean hands and a pure heart" may have a share in the worship of the true and living God.

The reference to the "root of bitterness" and to the immorality or irreligious nature of one like Esau (vss. 15-16) recalls what has already been said in chapters 3 and 4 with regard to the rebellion of Israel against God at the time of the Exodus. It is essentially such rebellion or disobedience which our author accounts to be man's chief sin (3:16-19). It is rebels who "fail to obtain the grace of God" (vs.15), and it is against such sin that the sons need to be warned that they may maintain proper direction along the Christian way of life.

Mount Zion and the Christian Way (12:18-24)

The author now gives the ultimate reason why the Christian's attitude is fundamentally different from that of a man like Esau. He has already suggested that the Christian should not be known for his "drooping hands" and "weak knees" (vs. 12), that his path always be made "straight" in order that the "lame" who accompany him might find it easy to walk in (vs. 13). This attitude, as we have seen, is contrasted with the "bitterness" which characterized Esau.

Justification for this exhortation lies in the fundamental differ-ence of spirit characterizing the Old Covenant and the New. The Old Covenant had been given at Mount Sinai under most terrify-ing conditions. The description of those conditions in verses 18-21 actually employs many of the very words of the Greek trans-lation of Exodus 19 and Deuteronomy 4 and 5. Little wonder

that the incident brought fear to the hearts of the Israelites when
even their leader remarked, "I tremble with fear" (vs. 21).

By contrast (vs. 22) the author places the New Covenant and
its confirmation at another mountain (Zion) and the city associated with it (Jerusalem). The origin of this idea no doubt goes
back to Isaiah 28:16:

> "Behold, I am laying in Zion for a foundation
>   a stone, a tested stone,
> a precious cornerstone, of a sure foundation:
>   'He who believes will not be in haste.' "

This thought and the accompanying one that the Messiah himself
will appear upon Mount Zion, having ridden through the gates of
the Holy City, is taken up in Isaiah 62:11 and Zechariah 9:9.
In turn, these become themes to be worked out in detail by various New Testament writers (Matt. 21:5; John 12:15; Rom. 9:33;
I Peter 2:6; and Rev. 14:1). The adjective "heavenly" which is
employed in connection with Jerusalem (vs. 22), however, makes
it clear that the author, as so often, is employing figurative language (see 4:16; 10:22).

The Mount Zion and "the city of the living God, the heavenly
Jerusalem" at which Christians have arrived is none other than
the "city which has foundations, whose builder and maker is God"
to which Abraham looked forward (11:10). *For Christians have
arrived.* In spirit they are already inhabitants of "the city of the
living God" and their companions are the "innumerable angels"
and the "assembly of the first-born," that is, all those who through
the centuries have in one way and another been God's true servants (vss. 22-23). "Assembly" is the ordinary Greek word for
"church." It might very well be translated "congregation," for the
reference is clearly to the people of God gathered together like a
mighty congregation and including those who through the centuries have turned away from a spirit of "bitterness," accepting
rather that fellowship which God holds out to man. The word
translated "first-born" is one which the New Testament employs
almost exclusively for Jesus Christ himself (Rom. 8:29; Col. 1:15,
18; Heb. 1:6; Rev. 1:5). Only in Luke 2:7 and Hebrews 11:28
is it used in the natural sense of the first child to be born into any
human family. The present passage, therefore, stands by itself in
New Testament usage and finds its meaning somewhere between
the natural usage of the word and its special application to Jesus

Christ. Christians are "first-born" in the sense that, reflecting the character of their Lord, they occupy a position of eminence among men; they are "just men made perfect," a really mature assemblage. This is the "communion of the saints"—the real people of God who know fellowship among themselves regardless of the barriers of time and place and rank, of color and race, which have separated men through the centuries.

The Christian's Call to an Unshakable Kingdom (12:25-29)

And now Hebrews returns to the thought of "a heavenly call" as issued to the readers, along with those under the Old Covenant, which was discussed in 3:6b—4:16. As before, there are very solemn terms warning of the danger of refusing "him who is speaking" to the Christian community (vs. 25). The argument, "if they did not escape . . . much less shall we escape" (vs. 25), is essentially that which was employed at 2:2-3 and 10:28-29. The reference in "him who warned them on earth" is obviously to Moses (10:28), while as surely he "who warns from heaven" is Jesus Christ. The latter is not a priest "on earth" as Moses and the descendants of Aaron his brother were (8:4), but is rather "from heaven" since it is there that his ministry is accomplished (8:2; 9:11-12). The quotation in verse 26 is from Haggai 2:6 and is evidently intended as a comprehensive statement, indicative of the universal and eternal character of the ministry of our Lord.

But the "kingdom" which Christians receive "cannot be shaken" (vs. 28). It is not transitory but eternal. The phraseology in the first part of this verse is striking for two reasons: first, because this is only the second reference to the "kingdom" to be found in the letter as a whole. The other appears at 1:8 in the quotation from Psalm 45:6-7. As we have seen, the major argument of Hebrews relates to the high priesthood of Jesus Christ. The present passage, however, linked as it is with the argument in 1:8, indicates that our Lord's kingship is never far from the author's mind. His high priesthood is based upon his sovereignty over the universe of which he is heir as Son (1:2). Second, the verse is significant because it speaks of Christians as "receiving" the kingdom, a term commonly employed in Judaism and carried over into the Christian Church. In Luke's Gospel, in fact, our Lord remarks to his "little flock": "It is your Father's good pleasure to give you the kingdom" (Luke 12:32). This saying occurs in Luke alone, but it follows immediately after the exhortation to "seek his kingdom" (vs. 31), which is found also in Matthew 6:33. In all of these passages, including that immediately before us, the thought is that of accepting the sovereignty of God over one's life. In this passage such acceptance of God's sovereignty is a precondition to man's offering "to God acceptable worship."

The Communal Life of God's People Outside the Gate (13:1-17)

There is quite clearly a change in tempo between the immediately preceding sections and the one which here lies before us. From 10:19 through 12:29 the author conceives of the Christian life in terms of movement. The community is on the march, and the stress is upon the "faith" that undergirds progress and the "hope" which fastens upon the goal at the end of the road. In the present section, on the other hand, our author views the Christian brotherhood in its settled communal life. The keynote of such communal existence is "love," and it is now "love" which is the dominant factor in the community and which determines its character and life.

Rapidly the author deals with six social relationships in which "love" should be the dominant motif. These include one's relations to (1) one's brother in the Christian community (vs. 1), (2) the stranger without (vs. 2), (3) those who are persecuted (vs. 3), (4) one's married partner (vs. 4), (5) possessions (vss. 5-6), and (6) Christian leaders (vss. 7, 17). Between verses 7 and 17 there is an interlude (vss. 8-16), dealing with the Christian's suffering with Jesus Christ "outside the gate."

In verses 1 and 2 two comprehensive words for "love" cover one's proper relationships with those both within and outside the Christian community—"brotherly love" and "hospitality to strangers." In the Greek there is quite clearly a play on these words, both of which are rarely used in the New Testament. The former, indeed, occurs elsewhere only in Romans 12:10; I Thessalonians 4:9; I Peter 1:22; and II Peter 1:7; while the latter is found only in Romans 12:13. Indeed, it is noteworthy that in Romans 12: 10-14, the two ideas of love toward those within and without the Christian community and endurance in the hour of persecution are present together in the mind of Paul as in that of the author of Hebrews. This fact may be coincidental, or it possibly suggests a knowledge of Romans on his part. In either case, the passages are one in testifying to a consciousness on the part of the Christian community of being a little island in the midst of a sea of paganism.

It is clear, however, that the situation of the readers of Hebrews is quite different from that of the readers of Romans 12. There the "strangers" are Christians, as verse 13 makes clear; here it is at least likely that the "strangers" are those outside the Christian community. The fact that "some have entertained angels unawares" refers to Abraham's experience as recorded in Genesis 18:1-8. Moreover, in Romans 12:14 it is Christians who are persecuted, whereas in the present passage there is no suggestion that "those who are in prison" and "those who are ill-treated" are Christians (vs. 3). It is a compassionate humanitarianism, springing from the Christian's sense of weakness which he shares with all those who are "in the body," that Hebrews has in mind.

The author's attitude toward the subjects of "marriage" and "money" in verses 4 and 5 is to be contrasted with the attitude of the Qumran sect as expressed in its scriptures. The asceticism practiced at Khirbet Qumran is in marked contrast with the author's injunction that "marriage be held in honor among all" (vs. 4). It is true that there was no compulsion on members of the sect to live a celibate life, and according both to Josephus and to the scrolls, there were those who lived a married life in the various cities and villages throughout Israel. Nonetheless, within the sect asceticism was the ideal. On the contrary, the Christian ideal, as expressed in verse 4, is that of a married state which is maintained on a high moral and spiritual level. It is the sexual aberrations of immorality and adultery which God will judge; married life itself is clearly recognized as normative and proper.

Similarly, unlike the Qumran sect, there is here no thought of adopting a communal view of one's possessions. Any who joined the monastic life of the community at Khirbet Qumran were compelled to surrender all of their wealth. For the writer of Hebrews, the Christian ideal is to keep one's life "free from love of money, and be content with what you have" (vs. 5). The Christian's attitude toward all things is to be motivated by the sense of God's providential care of his people (vss. 5-6; see Ps. 118:6).

The word translated "leaders" in verses 7, 17, and 24 is derived from the same stem that provides the Greek word elsewhere translated "governor" (for example, Matt. 10:18; Luke 20:20;

Acts 23:24). In verse 7 such "leaders" are defined as those
through whom "the word of God" had come to the readers. The
word is used in exactly the same way in Acts 14:12 with reference to the Apostle Paul, and in Acts 15:22 it is applied to Judas
and Silas, the two messengers sent by the church at Jerusalem to
the church at Syrian Antioch at the close of the Jerusalem Coun-
cil. Its use here, therefore, would suggest an early stage in the
history of the community addressed, when the organization was
still loose and discipline was not rigidly enforced. Possibly two
sets of such "leaders" are in view, the first consisting of the early
group who had evangelized the community at the beginning (vs.
7), and the second of more permanent "leaders" to whom submission was to be granted in view of the fact that they were
"keeping watch over your souls" (vs. 17).

Reference to the "leaders" through whom his readers have been
evangelized with "the word of God" leads the author again to
ponder upon the central message of the letter, and he repeats that
message now with a pertinent exhortation (vss. 8-16). Jesus
Christ, who is the center of the gospel message, is the eternal sacrifice for sin offered up, as we have seen, "to sanctify the people
through his own blood" (vs. 12; see 9:13-14; 10:10, 14, 29).
The "altar" on which he was sacrificed provides food for "grace"
which is not available to contemporary Judaism ("those who serve
the tent," vs. 10). Such food and such grace are sufficient for
Christians, who are, therefore, to put aside all "diverse and strange
teachings" with reference to foods which were supposed to benefit their adherents (vs. 9). What these teachings were we have no
certain way of knowing. Contemporary Judaism had many stipu-
lations derived from the Law and Pharisaic traditions with regard to "clean and unclean" meats or food. The Qumran sect also
had such teachings of its own. There is reference to something of
the sort also in the peculiarly gnostic teachings to which Paul
makes reference in Colossians 2:16-23.

The remark about Jesus' suffering "outside the gate" and the
consequent necessity that Christians should "go forth to him outside the camp, bearing abuse for him" (vss. 12-13) appears to reflect a time when the Christian community was faced with the
necessity of breaking away from the older Judaism with its center
in the holy city of Jerusalem. Christians "have no lasting city"
but, like their spiritual father Abraham, "seek the city which is
to come" (vs. 14; see 11:10, 16). Following the death of the

martyred Stephen, the Hellenistic-Jewish Christians were scattered
as a direct result of persecution arising in the mother city, Jerusalem (Acts 8:1). Also at the beginning of the First Jewish War
(A.D. 66), according to the early church historian Eusebius, the
members of the Jewish-Christian community escaped from the
city of Jerusalem and fled across the Jordan to Pella. In the light
of the teaching of Hebrews as a whole, however, it is probable that
neither of these two events is specifically referred to in the present passage. Rather, the author likely has in mind the necessary
cleavage being drawn between the Christian Church and contemporary Judaism, which was the natural result of the exclusive
high priesthood of the Son of God. Jewish Christians are not to
cling to or live in the Jewish side of their faith. Rather, as Jesus
himself was excluded from his people so they are to bear "abuse
for him" (vs. 13). The Christian's highest duty is to "offer up a
sacrifice of praise to God," praise which consists in witnessing to
"his name" in the world (vs. 15).

EPISTOLARY CONCLUSION
Hebrews 13:18-25

The epistolary conclusion contains a benediction, perhaps the
most beautiful to be found in the New Testament (vss. 20-21).
The term "God of peace," which is a Pauline phrase (Rom. 15:
33; 16:20; II Cor. 13:11; Phil. 4:9; I Thess. 5:23), means "the
God who brings peace or salvation"; "peace" in Hebrew is one
of the words which are the equivalent of "salvation" (Isa. 52:7).
The idea that God raised up "our Lord Jesus" is also a Pauline
idea (I Cor. 15:15), though not exclusively so (see Acts 2:24,
32). That Jesus is the "shepherd of the sheep" is an idea explicitly stated in John 10:2 and implied in Mark 6:34. It has numerous Old Testament associations, where God (Ps. 23:1), or
alternatively his Messiah (Micah 5:4), is declared to be the shepherd of his people. The benediction is essentially a prayer that God
will properly equip his "sons" so that they may do his will in the
manner set forth in the letter. This can come only "through Jesus
Christ."

In verse 22 the author defines his work as both "my word of
exhortation" and a letter written to his readers. This would seem
to suggest that the document is first of all a theological discussion,

and that in order to present it to his readers the author sent it to them, with perhaps an accompanying letter.

In closing he makes two references of a personal nature, one to Timothy, whom we know to have been close to Paul toward the end of his career while in prison (Phil. 1:1; 2:19; Col. 1:1), although there is no other account of Timothy's having suffered imprisonment. The author of Hebrews seems to be speaking out of personal knowledge of Timothy's movements. Hebrews also speaks of "those who come from Italy," possibly a reference to Hellenistic-Jewish Christians.

The letter closes with the brief prayer, "Grace be with all of you." In common with many of the New Testament letters the writer thus reminds his readers of the grace which binds them to one another and to God.

THE LETTER OF

JAMES

INTRODUCTION

Historical and Literary Problems

Authorship

Since early in the third century the Church has traditionally held that the "James" (Hebrew and Greek "Jacob") named
here was the brother of Jesus (Mark 6:3). He was for many years
the head of the church at Jerusalem (Acts 15:13-21), and should
not be confused with the son of Zebedee who was put to death
under Herod Agrippa I, about A.D. 46 (Acts 12:1-2). The name,
however, was a common one and it is notable that the author
merely describes himself as "a servant of God and of the Lord
Jesus Christ" (1:1). This has led to speculation that the work is
either pseudonymous (that is, written in the name of the Lord's
brother by someone wishing to issue the letter under the cloak of
his authority—an unlikely theory, since in such case the real
author would certainly have been at pains to indicate more specifically who the James intended was!) or else is by an unknown
James who was no more than he claims to be.

When certain characteristics of the book itself are examined,
these appear to many to be damaging to the traditional theory of
its authorship. For example, the author never quotes from the Old
Testament save in the form it assumes in the Greek translation
(Septuagint)—a fact not too damaging in itself, since he was
writing for Greek-speaking readers. But when to this fact is added
another—namely, that the Greek of this letter is some of the best
vernacular Greek to be found in the New Testament—it would
seem either that the author was quite familiar with Greek, or else
that he employed an amanuensis, and of this latter there is no
evidence. It is even thought that 1:17a is a hexameter line quoted
from a Greek author. It scarcely needs saying that James the
brother of Jesus, a Galilean by birth, would have spoken Aramaic

as did all Palestinian Jews in his day and would not likely have
been bilingual to the extent required by such evidence as this.

There are, however, certain facts to be placed on the other side
of the ledger: (1) the very lack of any attempt to designate his
status in his salutation (1:1) argues for the author's being someone
well known for his prestige and authority; (2) the only "James"
so qualifying was the Lord's brother, head of the Jerusalem church
(Acts 15) and a man no doubt of real ability, as his high station
would suggest; (3) numerous passages (1:2-4; 1:5-8; 1:9-11; 2:5,
9-13; 3:5-10; 3:18; 4:7-10; 4:11-12; 4:17; 5:1-6; 5:12) suggest that
the author was well acquainted with Jesus' teaching in the form it
early assumed, before the Gospels were written; indeed, 5:12
probably represents an accurate knowledge of the Aramaic idiom
used by Jesus, as Matthew 5:37 does not; (4) the stress on the
ethical implications of the gospel and the fact that it is termed
"the perfect law . . . of liberty" (1:25) are in accord with what
we should expect from a Hebraic-Jewish Christian like the head of
the Jerusalem church, as is the combination of prayer and forgiveness of sins with anointing and healing (5:13-15; see Mark
2:5); (5) numerous parallels have been pointed out between the
contents of the letter and the texts of the Qumran community
(1:2-8; 1:17; and others), a fact which would accord with the
writing of the letter in the context of the influence of and interest
aroused by the Qumran community settled so near to Jerusalem.

In the light of these considerations we may well assume that the
traditional authorship remains the best hypothesis proposed to
date. Exact knowledge is thus far unobtainable as to how far a
native of "Galilee of the Gentiles" like James may have been acquainted with the Greek language. If he wrote it even passably,
assistance from another who knew it as his native tongue would
have made it possible for him to eliminate Semitisms from his
manuscript, as the like authorship on a joint basis by "native" and
"foreigner" in modern languages serves to demonstrate.

Readers

If, as is suggested in the comment on 1:2-8, this piece of literature was first delivered as a sermon and afterward sent out to a
wider audience as a letter, it may well be that James' hearers were
Christians in Jerusalem. It is likely, however, that "the twelve
tribes in the dispersion" to whom it was sent out later included all
in the "new Israel of God," whether Jews or Gentiles.

This double reference of the letter in its final form, together with the character of the hearers whom James at first had in mind, would account for certain features that otherwise appear puzzling. Thus, while the letter is written in excellent vernacular Greek which at times approaches the literary style of the day and betrays little if any evidence of being "translation Greek," the condition of the church(es) addressed seems more applicable to those established among Jews in Jerusalem than among Gentiles. For their "assembly" the Greek word "synagogue" is employed (2:2), a term used of Christians nowhere else in the New Testament; and the presence of a rich man at the worship service is sufficiently rare to occasion considerable flurry—a phenomenon likely in Jerusalem where the early Jewish Christians were notably poor (Acts 24:17; Rom. 15:25-27; I Cor. 16:1-4; see the comment on James 2:6-7). Certain cultural features, too, suggest that a Jewish group was addressed, especially the injunctions relative to the treatment of the sick (5:13-15). As already mentioned, certain features of the teaching also suggest contact with the Qumran community. This would, of course, be the natural lot of the Jewish church in Jerusalem.

On the other hand, the statement that it is the rich "who blaspheme that honorable name" by which the readers are called (2:7) is reminiscent of the fact that "the disciples were for the first time called Christians" at Syrian Antioch (Acts 11:26; see I Peter 4:16). This verse might, therefore, represent a touch added for the wider circle of James' readers. These and like features of this little sermon-letter suggest a dual character of Jewish and Gentile hearers and readers such as might have been addressed by a Christian writer at any time after the inception of the Gentile mission of Paul.

Date

The letter has been assigned a very late date by interpreters who do not believe it to be the work of James the Lord's brother. By others it has been thought perhaps the earliest New Testament book, written even as early as A.D. 49. The late date is suggested largely by reason of the scarcity of evidence for its use. It is possible, however, that I Peter 1:1-2 contains the first turn of a phrase to show any leaning on James (1:1), in which case the letter might have been written shortly before A.D. 67 or even during that year. It could, however, be cogently argued that both letters draw upon the common stock of Christian phraseology employed by the Early Church in Jerusalem and might, accordingly, be given an identical date.

Accepting the authorship by James, we would place the composition of the letter in Jerusalem sometime before the opening of the First Jewish War (A.D. 66-70), possibly about A.D. 65. This would allow for James to have heard of the Judaizing objections to Paul's doctrine of justification by grace through faith (Rom. 3 and 4; Gal. 3) and for a desire on his part to correct the misinterpretation of Paul's writings (particularly Romans) thus involved (see 2:14-26).

The early center of the Christian faith had been Jerusalem (Acts 1-12), and the head of the church there would continue to think of it as the hub of all things Christian, with every other part of Christendom resulting from the Gentile mission qualifying as "dispersion" to his mind! Peter, following in Paul's steps to Rome, would have learned to see matters rather differently (I Peter 1:1-2). Perhaps we should see a hint of this attitude in the lack of any address in the letter attributed to James in Acts 15: 23-29 (see also 15:13, 19-21).

Contents

The theme of the letter, despite much writing to the contrary, appears to be *salvation* in several of its aspects. These include: salvation from the trials and temptations presented by life to the believer in Jesus Christ, the ethical implications for Christian living which such salvation entails, and the eternal aspects of salvation which one can either see or foresee on the historical plane.

OUTLINE

Salutation. James 1:1

Salvation from Life's Trials and Temptations. James 1:2-27

Faith—the Means or Way (1:2-8)
Salvation (the Crown of Life)—God's Gift (1:9-18)
God's Word—the Power (1:19-27)

Salvation's Implications for Social and Personal Living. James 2:1—5:6

Inconsistency of Faith with Partiality (2:1-13)
Relation of Faith to Works (2:14-26)
Opposition Between God's Word and Man's Word (3:1-18)
Opposition Between Passion and Humility (4:1—5:6)

Salvation in the Light of Eternity. James 5:7-20

Endurance Until the Lord's Coming (5:7-11)
Oaths and the Judgment (5:12)
Prayer and Healing (5:13-18)
Conversion of the Sinner (5:19-20)

COMMENTARY

SALUTATION
James 1:1

The salutation of the Letter of James more closely follows the usual format of a Greek letter of the day ("So-and-so to So-and-so, greetings") than any other of the New Testament letters. The word for "servant" really means "slave." Other New Testament writers employ this strong word about themselves and their attitude toward Christ (see Rom. 1:1; II Peter 1:1; Jude 1; Rev. 1:1). The idea is a prophetic one: God is man's only Lord and man is his servant (see Num. 11:11; Judges 2:8; Ps. 19:11; Isa. 42:1). It is striking that from the earliest times the Christian community ascribed to Jesus Christ the status of Lord, so giving him the status of "the LORD" (Yahweh) of the Old Testament (see Acts 2:36; I Cor. 12:3).

The address, "To the twelve tribes in the dispersion," could mean that James was writing only to Jews. But if so, he employed terminology outmoded long before his day, since the twelve tribes had long since ceased to exist. It is far more likely that, as was the custom of the Early Church, he adopted the terms of the Old Covenant to describe the Christian community under the New.

"Greeting" has been the common Greek salutation for centuries. It comes from the stem of a verb meaning to "rejoice" and is found in a number of related languages, including English. Our "cheer up" contains the same stem and gives a fairly accurate idea of the greeting's original meaning.

SALVATION FROM LIFE'S TRIALS AND TEMPTATIONS
James 1:2-27

The entire "letter," with the exception of its opening verse, may well be an essay or sermon. Possibly the author first composed it to serve this end and afterwards added the salutation and sent it forth to reach a larger audience than that for which it was originally composed. In any case, there is little in it to suggest that it was meant to meet a particular situation. It appears rather to be an essay on the general subject of "salvation" and the endurance required to attain it, particularly as the Christian is faced with the trials and temptations to which he is exposed in a secular culture.

The noun "salvation" does not occur in the letter, though the verb "to save" is fairly common (1:21; 2:14; 4:12; 5:15, 20). James thinks of salvation in terms of life or "the crown of life" (1:12), a figurative manner of speaking found also in Revelation 2:10. The two parts of the phrase also appear separately in the same sense in the New Testament (for "crown" or "wreath" see I Cor. 9:25; I Peter 5:4; and for "life" see John 1:4; Acts 11:18; Rev. 22:1). These terms with the same meaning of salvation also appear in the contemporary Jewish literature, for example, in the Dead Sea Scrolls.

Faith—the Means or Way (1:2-8)

The discussion of salvation begins with a brief notice of the faith upon which its attainment is based (vs. 3). James is quite realistic in his view of the world in which Christians live. It is a world full of "various trials" (vs. 2; the Greek word may be translated "temptations"), and these constitute a genuine "testing" of one's faith (vs. 3). The reader is reminded of Jesus' experience at this point, and possibly James had it in mind (see Matt. 4:1-11; Heb. 5:7-10). Both Paul and Hebrews think of Jesus as passing through obedience and suffering to maturity or perfection, in which condition he becomes the Savior of men (see Phil. 2:5-11). Similarly, with James the testing of the Christian's faith issues in "steadfastness" or stick-to-it-iveness, if it is endured (vs. 3; see Rom. 5:3-5). This in turn leads to his being "perfect and complete" (vs. 4; the words mean "mature" in our modern terminology, see Eph. 4:13; Heb. 6:1), that is, to his arriving at the goal that God sets for a man's life. That Christians should "count it all joy" when they are subjected to experiences which so closely parallel those of their Lord ought to be obvious. No Christian should expect life to be for him a bed of roses, when his Lord's was not (see Matt. 5:11-12; Rom. 6:1-4; Col. 1:24-29).

At the heart of Christian experience is a "wisdom" from above (vs. 5; 3:17) which makes it possible for the believer both to understand the nature of the gospel and to act in accordance with its demands. James is later to elaborate this theme (3:13-18). Here it is his purpose merely to assure his readers that it is God's gift and not to be acquired by one's natural effort. The God of the Christian is One "who gives to all men generously and without reproaching." This is in accord with Jesus' teaching (see Matt. 7: 7-11 and Luke 11:9-13).

The one condition on man's part upon which this gift of God rests is that faith of which James has been speaking (vs. 6). This again is an echo of Jesus' teaching (Matt. 21:22; Mark 11:24). It had found expression in his ministry of healing on numerous occasions (Mark 2:5; 5:34; 10:52; Luke 7:9). The Gospels record the fact that when the response of faith was not present Jesus was unable to perform his saving works (Mark 6:5-6).

To make faith rather than works the normative response of man toward God's revelation represents a Christian recovery of the prophetic teaching and is not to be found in the Jewish literature contemporary with the beginnings of the Christian Church. It represents a major stress of Paul (see Rom. 4; Gal. 3). It was accepted also in the earliest days of the Church (Acts 3:16; 6:5; 11:24). The comparison of one who "doubts" to "a wave of the sea that is driven and tossed by the wind" comes nearest to Paul's description of the doubter in Ephesians 4:14. The Greek word translated "double-minded" (vs. 7) is a natural description of a person characterized by ambivalence, one "unstable in all his ways."

Salvation (the Crown of Life)—God's Gift (1:9-18)

Not to Be Confused with One's Earthly Lot (1:9-11)

Like the Old Testament prophetic writings, the Christian faith early had much to say relative to a proper scale of values, and the Church followed its Master in an earnest endeavor to set men's minds right at this point. "Treasures on earth" were set over against "treasures in heaven" (Matt. 6:19-21), the carnal opposite the spiritual (I Cor. 3:1-4; see also Luke 16:19-31). The "rich man" would find it difficult "to enter the kingdom of God" (Mark 10:25), and the rich church would hear its Lord say, "I will spew you out of my mouth" (Rev. 3:16). This is not to say that the rich man would be condemned for his riches or the poor man accepted for his poverty. It was a mere matter of fact that "not many . . . wise according to worldly standards, not many . . . powerful, not many . . . of noble birth" had been chosen by

God to become members of Christ's Church (I Cor. 1:26-28). Outside Palestine, at least, most early Christians had previously been slaves (I Cor. 7:21-24; 12:13). The present passage and 2:2-7, however, suggest that a rich minority already were to be found in the Church.

James' present point, however, is that in the Christian brotherhood such distinctions do not count, for before the Lord of life they do not (see 2:5). It is true of the Christian who is rich, as of other rich men, that "like the flower of the grass . . . will the rich man fade away in the midst of his pursuits" (vss. 10-11). That "you can't take it with you" is no less applicable to the Christian than to another.

In the Christian brotherhood a point of view transcending such monetary distinctions is secured. There is in this fellowship a leveling process at work which results in "exaltation" for the "lowly brother," and equally in "humiliation" for "the rich" one. This teaching is identical with that of Paul (Gal. 3:28; Col. 3:11). But it also finds a real affinity with Isaiah 40:6-8, where the transitory nature of "all flesh" is contrasted with "the word of our God" which "will stand for ever." The thought of the creative and powerful "word of truth" is only a few verses away from this passage in James (vss. 18-21) and may have arisen from the association of ideas in the prophetic passage cited. But there are also parallels between James' teaching here and Jesus' parable of the Sower (Matt. 13:3-9), for example, "the sun . . . with its scorching heat," the withering of the grass, and the falling of its flower.

Assured by God's Loving Promise (1:12)

James now returns to the positive attitudes taken up in verses 2-4 with respect to trials or temptations. The comments made on the former passage apply in general to verse 12 as well.

Two new thoughts which appear to go beyond those in verses 2-4 are: (1) That the maturity spoken of in verse 12 is to be equated with receiving "the crown of life," that is, the *crown* which is *life*. In the contemporary culture a crown (chaplet, diadem) stood either for authority, as in the case of kings, or for achievement or victory, as in athletic contests (I Cor. 9:25) and in the "triumph" given to a returning conqueror. In the latter case, the crown was roughly the equivalent of a medal of distinction or an athletic cup with us. It is probably the latter idea that is present here; life is the crown or medal granted to him who attains matur-

ity, or, better, it is the maturity itself. (2) That "God has promised"
this crown "to those who love him" is also a new thought in the
letter. Its equivalent elsewhere is to be found only in Revelation
2:10, and there faithfulness rather than love is the condition of
the crown's reception. That God gives promises on this condition
is, however, a biblical idea (Exod. 20:6; Deut. 7:9).

Tempting Due to Covetousness (1:13-15)

It might be argued that, since God is the author of all things, he
also sends to men experiences of trial, of testing, of temptation
(vss. 2-4). Indeed, God does bring men into a situation of testing
with a view to discerning and even strengthening character. This
is one step in the maturing process. It is one thing, however, to
say that God brings a man into such a situation and quite another
to suggest that the test or trial is in itself the equivalent of the
temptation which may emerge from it. James is here arguing
against the pagan thought that opposites (good and evil) exist
side by side in God.

Like Paul (Rom 7:7-25), James sees the source of a man's
temptations to lie in "his own desire" (vs. 14, or "covetousness"),
which, given the testing situation, has "lured" and then "enticed"
him. Man's temptation comes from within, from what he is, not
from without. The scene is set by life's trials; but a man's response
to these—that which converts trials into temptations—depends
upon what the man himself is like within.

The sequence following in verse 15 of "desire," "sin," "death"
is also closely related to Paul's thought in Romans 7:8-10. In both
writers "death" is intended to cover every form of disintegration
and final collapse to which man is heir. Death was, indeed, the
opposite of life, and both alike related to every side of a man's
being (see Jer. 21:8).

Gift from God (1:16-18)

Having made it clear that God is not the author of man's temptations, James now turns to the contrary affirmation that God is
the author of his salvation. Verse 16 is a link between the two
thoughts and is a plea to the reader to think straight! God is not
to be charged with man's shortcomings. On the contrary, it is the
"good giving and the suitable gift" (see vs. 17, perhaps a well-
known poetic line), no matter what this may be, that is "from
above." Specifically, our new creation "by the word of truth" (see

I Peter 1:23; John 1:1-5) is from God, so we become the "first fruits" of a regenerated universe (Rom. 8:19-23; Rev. 14:4).

In the difficult clause, "with whom there is no variation or shadow due to change," James is perhaps mentally comparing God with the sun and other heavenly bodies which do exhibit changes and cast shadows.

God's Word—the Power (1:19-27)

Condition of Its Reception: Humility (1:19-21)

Having said that "the word of truth" is God's creative agency in man's redemption, James now goes on to declare what is required of man by way of response: "Receive with meekness the implanted word, which is able to save your souls" (vs. 21). But what is involved in meekness (humility), and how does it express itself? It involves being "quick to hear" (a good listener), "slow to speak" (thoughtful and deliberate), "slow to anger" (not over-hasty, given to jumping to conclusions), combined with the willingness to go into action when the wrong is shown to be one's own ("put away all filthiness and rank growth of wickedness"). All such response adds up to "the righteousness of God," that is, that which he requires of man (Matt. 5:20; 6:33).

Manner of Its Use: Obedience (1:22-25)

Humility can go too far. It can declare that one is worthy only to sit and listen, but not to act. People who have this attitude deceive themselves (vs. 22). This is like Paul's teaching in Romans 2:13. It was common Jewish teaching in his day. Such self-deceived people (those who practice false humility) are compared with the man who takes a quick look at a mirror and goes away, forgetful of the kind of man he is (the point being, he should have done something about it!). By contrast, the Christian should look "into the perfect law, the law of liberty" (that is, "the word of truth," or the gospel) as his mirror. Seeing himself in its light, he should not forget what he is like but be "a doer that acts" (vs. 25; see II Cor. 3:18).

Summary of Its Message: Social and Personal Ethics (1:26-27)

But what action is to be taken by the well-intentioned Christian? And what is to be identified with true religious practice?

Religion must be given some solid content. James' positive definition is in terms of social and personal ethics. He gives, for the
moment, two examples—"to visit orphans and widows in their
affliction," a deep need to which the Early Church had long re-
sponded (Acts 6); and "to keep oneself unstained from the world,"
a teaching especially important as the Church went out into the
profligacy of the Greco-Roman society of its day (Gal. 1:4; Eph.
2:2).

SALVATION'S IMPLICATIONS FOR SOCIAL AND PERSONAL LIVING

James 2:1—5:6

Inconsistency of Faith with Partiality (2:1-13)

Distinctions Based on Wealth (2:1-4)

That true religion, or what James now calls "the faith of our
Lord Jesus Christ," may be defined in terms of its ethical implications is further illustrated by a hypothetical case of partiality practiced in the church. The example concerns two men—one rich,
the other poor—who attend the "assembly" (literally, "synagogue,"
either gathering, congregation, or house of worship) of the Christian community. One man wears gold rings and fine clothing, the
other is shabby. The assembled congregation is assumed to be impressed by the magnificence of the one and to treat him with
great deference, while perversely ignoring the other or treating him
with disrespect. One gains the impression that an actual practice
in the church is being described! This seems to follow particularly
from the wording in verse 4, where the Greek may mean, "Do you
not customarily make distinctions among yourselves?"

The description of Jesus Christ as "the Lord of glory" represents a pinnacle of the Christian teaching regarding his person.
As the Christian's Lord, Jesus is here identified with the "glory"
or manifested presence of God among his people (I Sam. 4:22;
Isa. 6:3; John 1:14).

Argument Against Such Practice (2:5-13)

The first point in a detailed argument against partiality is that
God, if he discriminates at all, does so in favor of the "poor in

the world" rather than against them! Verse 5 sounds like a curious blending of the teaching of Jesus (Matt. 5:3; Luke 12:32) with that of Paul (I Cor. 1:26). (For the end of the verse see the comment on 1:12.)

In verses 6 and 7 it seems that the examples of both rich and poor are strangers, unknown to the local Christian congregation. James now advances the argument, therefore, that the rich as a class have an unsavory reputation in view of their treatment of Christians (vss. 6-7). And this is true on two counts: (1) they oppress Christians, dragging them into court (see Acts 4:1-3; 13:50), and (2) they blaspheme the name of Christ. The rhetorical questions are intended to lead to the conclusion that the burden of proof is on the rich stranger to show why he should expect respect at the hands of Christians!

James accepts, as did the whole Church (Matt. 22:39; Rom. 13:9-10), the high teaching of Leviticus 19:18, to the effect that love is the fundamental attitude to be cultivated toward other persons. He terms this law a "royal" one (vs. 8), no doubt meaning that it is addressed not to slaves but rather to free men judged to be sovereign in governing their own lives (1:25; 2:12; I Peter 2:9).

The final argument against partiality is derived from a conception of the Law as a unit; so that "whoever keeps the whole law but fails in one point has become guilty of all of it" (vs. 10). This is a principle accepted also by Jesus and Paul (Matt. 5:19; Gal. 3:10), as apparently by their Jewish contemporaries. The application of the principle to the Law's specific commands was easy enough to understand (vs. 11). The difficulty lay in observing that an attitude such as partiality was also to be comprehended under the Law's jurisdiction; so that anyone exhibiting this attitude committed sin and was "convicted" as a transgressor (vs. 9). In suggesting that attitudes and motives come under the Law's jurisdiction, James adopts much the position of Jesus in the Sermon on the Mount (Matt. 5:22, 28, 39). Both apply the principle to love of neighbor. The law which James would thus place before the Christian conscience is "the law of liberty" (that is, "the word of truth," or the gospel—1:18). This Christian law may be said to limit its concern to items in which man is free to exercise his conscience and judgment. It derives no doubt from Jesus' limitation of the Law to the motive of love toward God and neighbor (Matt. 22:34-40). The argument relating to partiality is finished as it was begun, with a reference to God's attitude (vs. 13). God's example, of mercy which "triumphs over judgment," is in this, as in all matters, man's true guide.

Relation of Faith to Works (2:14-26)

The latter part of chapter 2 has been held by some to have been written in opposition to Paul's teaching on justification by grace through faith alone (Rom. 4; Gal. 3). Luther went so far as to call this "a right strawy epistle." Admittedly, both writers employ the example of Abraham, apparently to prove opposite points (vs. 21; Rom. 4:2-25). But on closer examination, it is clear that they are employing the same terms with different meanings. "Faith" with Paul is saving faith, intimate attachment to Christ issuing naturally in fruitage such as he wishes (Rom. 4:19-22; Gal. 3:14 with 5:22-23); with James "faith" is "faith by itself" (vs. 17), that is, shallow belief in a proposition, such as "demons" may have (vs. 19). Similarly, when Paul speaks of "works" in this connection, he means "works of the law," legal righteousness performed to secure salvation (Gal. 3:2); but James by "works" means the natural product of true faith—what Paul calls "the fruit of the Spirit" (Gal. 5:22). In consequence, there can be no real conflict between Paul and James at this point, though one may have written to correct a misunderstanding caused by the writing of the other.

Futility of Faith without Works (2:14-17)

"Faith but . . . not works" (vs. 14), or "faith by itself" (vs. 17), is the subject of James' interest in this section and the next. Such faith is "dead" or futile and therefore cannot be true Christian faith. Christian faith is a working faith, one that follows through and gets results. The single illustration at this point is that of the poor brother or sister in need of food or clothing. To say to such a one, "Go in peace, be warmed and filled" (vs. 16), is sheer mockery. It accomplishes nothing. Such faith is obviously dead; it is equally obviously not Christian. For everything Christian is on the side of life and produces life and issues in the crown of life.

Faith with and without Works (2:18-26)

The hypothetical opponent who wishes to separate faith and works, suggesting that a man may have the one without the other, may be a Jew, if we may interpret James' words as, "You (a Christian) have faith and I (a Jew) have works," meaning thereby that the two faiths may well agree to disagree at this point. In any case, the reply is to the effect that though his opponent may accept such a division as valid, the Christian cannot. Anything worthy of the name of "faith," to the Christian's mind, can never exist "apart from . . . works." Take by way of example the proposition that "God is one" (vs. 19). Here is something that might conceivably be called a "faith apart from . . . works"; for it certainly is nonproductive. But of what worth is it? "Even the demons" have such faith! By having it, they invalidate it.

No, says James, faith and works go together and are not to be separated. Indeed, "I by my works will show you my faith" (vs. 18). To demonstrate this, James takes first the case of Abraham's willingness to offer up Isaac. Here clearly "faith was active along with his works, and faith was completed by works." Such faith demonstrated itself in its activity, so much so that one may say that "a man is justified by works and not by faith alone" (vs. 24). The same conclusion appears justified in the case of Rahab the harlot, who assisted the spies at the capture of Jericho (Joshua 2:1-21). Hers surely was a working faith (see also Heb. 11:31).

In conclusion, James calls upon the well-known Hebrew-Christian teaching that body and spirit cannot be divided one from the other (vs. 26); both are needed to form the unity of man's being. So, he declares, faith and works must go together; without the one, the other is dead.

Opposition Between God's Word and Man's Word (3:1-18)

Man's Need of Controlling His Word (3:1-2)

The Christian's works must measure up at every point. There is one member of a man's body which has a vastly important part to play in the activity of "the whole body," namely, his *tongue*. So far is this true that "if any one makes no mistakes in what he says he is a perfect man, able to bridle the whole body also." Control of the tongue is, in other words, the true mark of maturity in the Christian. It is only such persons who should undertake to become teachers, for the teacher is one who is "judged with greater strictness" regarding what he says.

Examples of Small Controllers (3:3-4)

The reader is not to look askance at the tongue because it is so small a member. Size has nothing to do with significance here. Two comparable examples are offered from other fields of human interest. These are the bits which are placed in the mouths of horses (vs. 3), and the very small rudder used in guiding a ship (vs. 4). In each case, the "whole bodies" of the horses and the whole ship are properly directed and controlled.

The Tongue—a Small Uncontrolled Controller (3:5-12)

Similarly, "the tongue is a little member" and, if the analogy held, it should be capable of controlling for good man's whole body. Instead, there is present here a factor which is absent in the cases of bits and rudder just cited. This factor, though James does not here employ the term, is sin. Man can tame everything else with which he has to do—beast, bird, reptile, sea creature, but not the tongue; it is "a restless evil, full of deadly poison," "a fire," "an unrighteous world among our members." The tongue, instead of controlling for good, succeeds only in "staining the whole body." Being itself "set on fire by hell," it kindles the entire "cycle of nature," the cycle of man's whole existence from morning to night.

James is particularly impressed by the tongue's double-dealing, its "blessing and cursing" at the same time, the blessing being for God, the cursing for men.

The implication of the passage is that the same attitude of respect and love must be maintained both for God and for "men, who are made in the likeness of God." This is the equivalent of Jesus' teaching relative to the only two necessary commandments; the command to love one's fellow men is placed on a par with loving God (Mark 12:31-33). Throughout this section, moreover, there are subtle reminiscences of the Sermon on the Mount. The question emerges here, therefore, as to whether James may not have had available the teaching of Jesus in some oral-tradition form. Obviously, he is not merely quoting from one of our canonical Gospels.

The phrase "the Lord and Father" in verse 9 has no exact equivalent in Scripture. The nearest to it is perhaps Paul's favorite phrase, "the God and Father of our Lord Jesus Christ" (Rom. 15:6; II Cor. 1:3; Eph. 1:3).

Wisdom from Above (3:13-18)

Like the Old Testament and apocryphal "wisdom literature," James now traces both the tongue, and the word which it utters, back to two possible sources, to each of which he gives the general name of "wisdom." One of these sources is "the wisdom from above," the other in origin and nature is "earthly, unspiritual, devilish." James has already shown that the first of these is not natural to man but is to be acquired only from "God, who gives to all men generously and without reproaching" (1:5). Obviously, then, to James' mind such wisdom is to be identified with God's word, "the word of truth" (1:18), which we have seen to be the mediating cause of man's salvation (1:21). This divine wisdom James describes in remarkable fashion in terms of its effects—it is "first pure, then peaceable, gentle, open to reason, full of mercy and good fruits, without uncertainty or insincerity" (vs. 17), a description obviously motivated by James' endeavor to paint in vivid colors a picture contrasting sharply with what passes for wisdom among false teachers. The true teacher, infused with this divine wisdom, will "show his works in the meekness of wisdom," that is, in a sort of divinely instilled humility which will never prove "false to the truth" which he professes.

By contrast, the opposite kind of wisdom—which, since James feels impelled to write about it, must have already appeared in the Christian community—springs out of man's selfish nature. It manifests itself in "jealousy and selfish ambition" (vss. 14, 16), not in the wish to set forth God's truth but rather in an attempt to acquire a sort of personal corner on truth. In the end, this results in a man's being actually "false to the truth," as he boasts of his own relation to it. Among such teachers the net product is naturally "disorder and every vile practice." This section on the conflict between the two words is closed with what again sounds like a reference to the oral tradition of Jesus' teachings—"the harvest of righteousness is sown in peace by those who make peace" (vs. 18; see Matt. 5:9-10). That is to say, the righteousness which God expects of man is achieved only by those who exercise the divine wisdom in humility and peace, never by those who exalt their own wisdom and so achieve nothing but disorder.

Opposition Between Passion and Humility (4:1—5:6)

Friendship with the World (4:1-4)

The contrast between the two kinds of wisdom which James has drawn in the above section, he now discusses on the emotional level. The causes of wars and fightings in which the natural man apart from God—what he calls "the world" (vs. 4)—indulges are man's own "passions." These are the natural impulses which arise in man's "members" (that is, within the structure of his person), and which are actually "at war" within him. Like Paul, who speaks of "the law of sin which dwells in . . . [one's] members" (Rom. 7:23) and of the consequent conflict between "flesh" and "mind" that ensues (Rom. 7:25), James believes that the natural man or "the world" apart from God's grace is in an ambivalent condition from which he cannot of himself escape.

James' description of this hopeless state of "the world" is exceedingly graphic—"you desire and do not have," "you kill"; "you covet and cannot obtain," "you fight and wage war"; "you ask and do not receive" (a casual reference perhaps to Jesus' teaching as in Matt. 7:7, but in reverse) "because you ask wrongly." "Unfaithful creatures" in the Greek is "adulteresses"—a description of those who practice "friendship with the world" and one first given them by the Hebrew prophets (Hosea 3:1). And as with those prophets, James sees no compromise at this point: "friendship with the world is enmity with God" (see Matt. 6:24).

Friendship with God (4:5-10)

There is, however, a different emotional attitude which brings real joy and peace to the human heart, the attitude of the man who does not insist on his own desires but rather submits to God, draws near to God, humbles himself before the Lord. This, too, is akin to Paul's teaching to the effect that men must "yield . . . [themselves] to God . . . and . . . [their] members to God as instruments of righteousness" (Rom. 6:13), and both teachings are akin to that of Jesus (Matt. 6:33). It is only out of such genuine humility before the Lord that a sense of exaltation arises (vs. 10; see Luke 14:11).

This is always true of man's experience, because fundamentally he is dealing with a God who "yearns jealously over the spirit which he has made to dwell in us" (vs. 5; Exod. 20:5). God desires fellowship with man but on his own terms, and these terms are well expressed in Proverbs 3:34 which James quotes: "God opposes the proud, but gives grace to the humble" (vs. 6; see Luke 18:9-14). In verses 7-9 James gives us, in what amounts to "blank verse," his concise formula for achieving this fellowship with God and its consequent rich reward (compare Ps. 24:4; Matt. 5:4, 8). Much of this passage has the ring of Jesus' teaching, and, like the Sermon on the Mount, it exhibits the Hebrew poetic form of parallelism.

Judgment of Others (4:11-12)

James has already written against the practice, observable in the Church, of making distinctions between brothers on the basis of wealth (2:2-4). He now speaks out, and with great vigor, against speaking evil against and judging a brother at all. We are strongly reminded of Jesus' teaching on this subject (Matt. 7:1-5). The argument against such practice is carried to its logical conclusion—that when one disobeys the law relating to love of brothers one is actually calling in question the validity of the law itself, one so to speak "judges the law," setting himself above it. But God alone is both "lawgiver and judge."

Boasting (4:13-17)

In this and the following sections James returns to the arrogant rich (see 2:6-7), first to condemn their arrogance and then to proclaim their evil end. The actions of the rich are described in much the same manner adopted by Jesus in the parable of the Rich Fool (Luke 12:16-21). In both, the rich man is made to appear totally oblivious to the evanescent aspect of life and riches. He speaks within his heart and acts accordingly, as though life were to run on indefinitely, instead of being "a mist that appears for a little time and then vanishes" (vs. 14; see Ps. 90:5-6). This is the attitude of the practical materialist, whatever his protestations of religion may be. His boastful arrogance (vs. 16) for all practical purposes disregards the existence of the Lord of life in whose hands are all its issues (vs. 15).

The clause "If the Lord wills" (vs. 15), followed by some deduction based on this premise, is one commonly employed among both pious Jews and Moslems to this day. Its use represents the speaker's wish to indicate at every possible opportunity his sense of dependence on the divine mercy and no doubt may, contrary to James' intention, become merely a stereotyped formula indicative of a legalistic religion.

Worldly Riches (5:1-6)

The statement that the rich "have killed the righteous man" (vs. 6), taken literally, shows that in this passage, at any rate, James cannot be thinking of Christians. Doubtless he has in mind here the unconverted rich man (Jew or pagan) about whom he has already written (2:6-7), although that there were rich persons in the Christian community at the time of this writing has already been indicated (1:10; 2:2). Other features in the description of these rich also indicate outsiders, reflecting the preaching of both Hebrew prophets and Jesus. It had been a point of great importance in the Mosaic Law that "the wages of a hired servant" should be paid him at the end of each day's labor (Lev. 19:13). This was of no little practical necessity in a day when such laborers "lived from hand to mouth"; if a man's wages were kept back at the end of the day, he and his family did not eat (Deut. 24:14-15; Mal. 3:5; Matt. 10:10). It may be such a practice that James has in mind in verse 4. Then, too, the general attitude of these rich toward their rich garments, their gold and silver, their luxury and pleasure, suggests that they are practical materialists who have not learned the Christian attitude toward worldly values. Two outstanding characteristics of this teaching should be noted: First, it reflects quite clearly Jesus' teaching relative to "treasures on earth" and "treasures in heaven" (Matt. 6:19-21). The references to moth and rust as corrupting forces are significantly repeated in James (vss. 2-3), as though he were acquainted with the oral tradition of Jesus' teaching current at the time. The idea that rust will eat the rich man's "flesh" (that is, his person) as well as his silver and gold is akin to Paul's teaching about the body in I Corinthians 6:12-13. In all three—Jesus, Paul, and James—it is what a man's attachment to material values and pleasures does to his person (body, flesh) that is of deep concern. Second, James' teaching reflects the Early Church's awareness of the Last Judgment and of living in the end of time (see especially vss. 1, 3, 5; compare Heb. 1:2; I Peter 1:5; I John 2:18).

SALVATION IN THE LIGHT OF ETERNITY

James 5:7-20

Endurance Until the Lord's Coming (5:7-11)

This closing section of the letter focuses attention upon the eternal order. James has already written of the "one lawgiver and judge" of men (4:12). That one is now identified with the Lord who is about to come again. His coming is at hand; as Judge he "is standing at the doors" (vs. 9; see Matt. 24:33; Rev. 3:20). This idea of the nearness of the Lord's coming was a general belief of the Early Church (for example, see Phil. 4:5; I Thess. 4:15; I Peter 4:7; I John 2:18).

No doubt there were those in the Church who accepted such teaching in most literal fashion; indeed, there is some evidence to show that this was the case. Paul appears to have written I Thessalonians 5:1-11 in order to counsel the Church that nothing definite could be known about the matter of "times" and "seasons." Second Peter 3:8-10 suggests that, as Psalm 90:4 teaches, God's ways of reckoning time are not man's. The thought in both these passages would suggest that the prophetic minds in the Church interpreted any reference to time in the most general sense. Man must always be ready and waiting for the Lord of life. So also for James, man must, like the farmer, "be patient"; like the prophets and Job he must be "steadfast," ready to exemplify the same "suffering and patience" as they; and this in view of the fact that the Lord of life who is man's Judge is "compassionate and merciful" and will judge men accordingly when he comes.

Oaths and the Judgment (5:12)

The taking of an oath during ordinary conversation was a long-standing custom within the Hebrew-Jewish tradition, as it is in the Moslem world today. The idea was that one was converted from being a liar into a truth-teller by simply taking an oath by whatever one held sacred. James follows his Lord in teaching that truth is to be respected for its own sake, that "a man's word should be as good as his bond," his "yes be yes," his "no be no" (see Matt.

5:33-37). All this, again, is to be seen in the light of eternity, of the final Judgment, of God's "condemnation."

Prayer and Healing (5:13-18)

There was to James' mind, as to that of the Early Church generally, a very thin line of demarcation between history and eternity; the second could at any moment break upon the first. Nowhere is this seen more clearly than in the matter of sickness and health; both are to be taken before God—the one in petition, the other in praise. Verse 13 sounds like an intentional couplet in blank verse, thus:

> Is any among you ill? let him pray.
> Is any well? let him sing.

The verb translated "is . . . ill" above is the equivalent of the noun "suffering" in verse 10. It has a wide usage, but in verse 14 James clearly defines the "suffering" he means here as "sickness." In such a case, James suggests that "the elders of the church" be called in, that they may do two things: pray over the sick one, and anoint him with oil "in the name of the Lord." It was standard procedure in the Jewish community thus to combine prayer with anointing with oil. Wine was also used along with oil for medicinal purposes among the Jews (Luke 10:29-37). Such prayer by the elders is a special case of what is generally termed "intercessory prayer" today. Such prayer for others is based on the fact of the corporate nature of human life—a principle recognized everywhere throughout Scripture. As God deals with men in all matters on both an individual and a corporate level, there appears to be no reason why prayer should be an exception to this rule. It is clear from the phrases employed ("in the name of the Lord," "the prayer of faith," and "the Lord will raise him up") that James attributed the actual healing, not to the oil, but to the Lord. In Hebrew thought a man's person was a unit and both good and evil impinged upon that person as a whole, if at all. The righteous man whose "prayer . . . has great power in its effects" is the man committed to God's will, who prays for what his Lord wills and whose prayer is in consequence answered (Matt. 6:9-13; Mark 11:24-25; Rom. 8:26-27).

Conversion of the Sinner (5:19-20)

The last short section contains a further elaboration of the principle of corporate living already stated in verse 16. This is personal evangelism directed toward one in the Christian community who "wanders from the truth" of the gospel (1:18, 21-22). The soul saved from death in verse 20 is undoubtedly that of the sinner, not that of the evangelist; and if so, the "multitude of sins" thereby covered will surely also refer to those of the sinner. "Cover" is a Hebraism meaning "overlook," "forgive" (Ps. 32:1). First Peter 4:8 contains much the same thought. James' interest here and in the preceding section centers at all times in the sinner or the unhealthy person involved. His intense desire is to further personal evangelism, with a view to that sinner's conversion and restoration to Christian living.

THE FIRST LETTER OF

PETER

INTRODUCTION

Historical and Literary Problems

Authorship

There has been considerable doubt on the part of numerous New Testament interpreters concerning the identity of the author of the letter. This doubt has been strengthened by a study of the contents of First Peter itself. The Greek of the letter is of high quality, even classical in its expression at times. Its style, syntax, and extensive vocabulary (63 Greek words not found elsewhere in the New Testament) are those of a writer who used the Greek language with fluency and ease. Accordingly, the question arises whether a Galilean fisherman could have been the author of such a work. Admittedly, Galilee was a bilingual or even trilingual district to an extent, and Greek loan words have been found in the Palestinian Aramaic of the period. But this is far from saying that a Galilean fisherman could have written the smooth Greek of First Peter.

A further objection to the Petrine authorship occurs in connection with 4:16: "If one suffers as a Christian, let him not be ashamed, but under that name let him glorify God." This language, it is held by some, refers to the *official* Roman persecutions. Unofficial persecution, however, had always been a possibility with which the follower of Jesus had to reckon. To suffer under the name of "Christian" was possible at least as early as Acts 11:26; it became the actual experience of Paul and his associates. It is by no means clear that the readers of First Peter were suffering from an official persecution conducted by the state, rather than from the sort of occasional "hostility" such as was often stirred up against Christians by both Jewish and Gentile enemies (see Acts 5:41; 9:16; 15:26; Phil. 1:29).

On the other hand, as has frequently been pointed out, there are numerous subtle indications in First Peter that serve to identify its author with the Apostle of that name. First, although he generally quotes (with a fair degree of accuracy) from the Greek Old Testament (rather than from the Hebrew), this is merely what we should expect of one writing to churches in the Roman Empire whose Old Testament would ordinarily be the ancient Greek translation. What strikes one as most important in his quotations is the independence of the author's judgment in his selections and the insight which he shows into the possible Christian use of Old Testament passages not otherwise quoted in the New Testament (compare, for example, 1:16 with Lev. 11:44-45 and 19:2; 2:24-25 with Isa. 53:5-6; 3:14-15 with Isa. 8:12-13; 4:18 with Prov. 11:31; 5:7 with Ps. 55:22). In a number of these and like passages he is not so much consciously quoting as merely articulating his thought with the language of the Old Testament, thereby indicating that he had deeply steeped himself in those Scriptures. Second, the author's reference to himself as "a witness of the sufferings of Christ" (5:1) reflects the attitudes of an early period, when the Cross and Resurrection were the important themes of the Church's preaching rather than the events of Jesus' life and ministry (see Acts 2:22-36). Third, the injunction to "tend the flock of God" (5:2) may be a recollection of John 21:15-17, and similarly "clothe yourselves . . . with humility" (5:5) is possibly an allusion to John 13:4-5. Finally, there are numerous similarities between the teachings of the letter and those of Peter in the Book of Acts (see comment).

The problem of authorship is greatly relieved if we assume that "Silvanus" (5:12) was more than a mere messenger by whom Peter sent the letter to the churches addressed. In saying that "by Silvanus" he had "written briefly" to these churches, "exhorting and declaring that this is the true grace of God," Peter may wish to declare his colleague as coauthor of the letter. It had been Paul's custom to indicate coauthorship at the beginning of his letters, and in fact he had thus associated Silvanus with himself in the writing of First and Second Thessalonians (see 1:1 in each case). This Silvanus is in all probability the "Silas" of Acts (see comment on 5:12). And if so, he was a man of considerable stature in the Christian community (Acts 15:22-40), and one who was of great assistance to Paul, who was, like himself, both a Roman citizen (Acts 16:37) and a man of culture who could deal with the intelligentsia (17:4).

This theory of coauthorship, particularly if it be assumed that Peter merely gave Silvanus a somewhat general briefing on what he wished to write and then allowed him considerable freedom both in the matter of particular ideas to be included and the general structure of the letter, would perhaps account for several other phenomena which are to be noted. These are: first, the numerous similarities in vocabulary and style between First Peter on the one hand, and First and Second Thessalonians on the other; second, Peter's comprehensive injunction that Christians are to "be subject for the Lord's sake to every human institution" (2:13), as well as his further elaboration of this idea in connection with the honoring of "the emperor" in 2:13, 17 (Silvanus and Paul as Roman citizens would naturally be sensitive on this point in a way that the Galilean disciples would not); third, Silvanus' wide familiarity with both the Jewish and Greek cultures which prompted the Jerusalem church to appoint him as one of its two delegates to handle the delicate situation which had arisen in the church at Syrian Antioch (Acts 15:22, 27, 32-33) and which would admirably account for the many similarities to be noted between First Peter and Hebrews. These similarities reflect a wide knowledge of Christian doctrine and also of contemporary Jewish teaching. Although it is probable that the letter represents the joint labors of Peter and Silvanus, throughout the comment the author will be designated as "Peter" and singular pronouns will be employed.

Readers of the Letter and the Circumstances Involved

The readers are termed "exiles of the Dispersion in Pontus, Galatia, Cappadocia, Asia, and Bithynia" (1:1). The phrase "exiles of the Dispersion" relates, not to Jews, but rather to Christians generally (see comment on 1:1). Moreover, if we may assume that Silvanus joined Peter as coauthor, then there is no reason why the territory indicated should not include both Paul's field of labor and that of his colleague, Peter, since Silvanus labored with Paul throughout this area (Acts 15:40—18:5). Indeed, there is no assurance that Peter himself had preached to any great extent among the churches addressed (see I Peter 1:12). The Roman provinces named include practically the whole of Asia Minor, in any case the whole of the region lying north and west of the Taurus Mountains.

The order of the names suggests that the coauthors began with the provinces to the north and east, and then worked around clockwise in a circle to the more cultured and central ones to the west, and thus included the whole of Asia Minor.

Throughout the region specified there was a great mixture of races and cultures, including the old native peoples, as well as cultured Greeks and Orientals who, together with many Jews, had "infiltrated" the populous cities and towns. It was a region seething with heterogeneous elements, culturally, religiously, socially, and politically. Into this maelstrom of cultural elements came the Christian Church, brought there by those "who preached the good news" to all and sundry (1:12). It is quite likely that, as in other places in the Roman Empire, the Christian communities thus established were made up of all elements of the population, including Jews and Gentiles. That these Christian communities had been established not long before appears from the fact that the authors speak of them as "like newborn babes" and commend to them "the pure spiritual milk" which will lead them to "grow up to salvation." They were, however, already suffering persecution for their faith (1:6; 3:13-17; 4:12-19). Many Christians in the early period were actually slaves, and it is quite likely that the trials indicated were of a type such as Christian slaves might expect from pagan masters (see 2:18-23).

Date and Place of Writing

Those who believe that this letter contains distinct reference to a persecution conducted in the name of the Roman state, generally incline to the belief that it was written (1) about A.D. 67 and shortly after the Neronian persecution; or (2) if it be held that Peter was not the author, then during the Domitian persecution of A.D. 95; or (3) even at the time of the persecution under Trajan in A.D. 111-112. If, however, we accept the Peter-Silvanus authorship of the letter, we must settle on a date sometime before Peter's death in the late 60's. As it is generally agreed that Peter employed Paul's Letter to the Romans (A.D. 56-58) and other of the Pauline letters, the date is brought within the narrow compass of some ten years. If further it is agreed that First Peter was acquainted with Hebrews (whose date we have placed at A.D. 65 or 66), then the extreme limits for the date of the letter are restricted between A.D. 66 and 70. The year A.D. 67 meets all the requirements.

It is rather generally agreed that the reference in 5:13 to the one "at Babylon" is to the church at Rome, and, in consequence, that the letter was written from the capital city.

The Message and Composition of the Letter

First Peter is directed to new converts (2:2), encouraging them to achieve the purification or sanctification which is demonstrated by the putting away of "the passions of the flesh," a course which the Christian community approved as "good conduct among the Gentiles" (2:11-12). It is likely that it incorporates a manual of catechetical instruction for such new converts (1:3—4:11), either prepared by the Church and adopted by the coauthors of the letter or else prepared by them and others for this purpose. The elements of this catechetical manual as presented in First Peter show many similarities to elements in First and Second Thessalonians and other Pauline letters, as well as in James. It is further suggested that two hymns have been incorporated into this catechetical manual, one at 2:4-10 and the other at 3:18-22 (see also I Tim. 3:16).

Assuming that readers have experienced the new birth at baptism and will acknowledge the power which is now at work within them, the authors arrange most of their materials in the form of an exhortation, presenting the doctrine of sanctification in a highly developed form. Such sanctification, they say, is the content of the good news, the "living hope" of "an inheritance which is imperishable, undefiled, and unfading" (1:3-4, 12). The holy life to which such sanctification naturally leads is one patterned after the nature of God (1:13-17) and is generated in the Christian by "the living and abiding word of God" (1:22-25). This holy life is incarnated in the Church or Christian community (2:4-10) and exhibits a kind of "good conduct" among the Gentiles which cannot be overlooked by them (2:11-12), as it issues in right social relationships in every direction (2:13—3:12). Furthermore, this sanctified living can withstand the fires of persecution, for it begins with making Christ the sole Lord of one's life (3:13-17) and therefore is prepared to share his sufferings and glory (3:18—4:19).

Both Hebrews and First Peter were written by authors who for the moment at least were concerned to state the Christian doctrine of salvation against the background of cultic worship. Both speak of purification or sanctification, atoning sacrifice, priesthood, and "a spiritual house" for the true worship of God in which "spiritual sacrifices acceptable" to him may be offered. These many similarities between the two letters by no means require that we suppose their authors to have collaborated. They do, however, suggest a common interest and even possibly the use of one letter by the other writer.

OUTLINE

Salutation. I Peter 1:1-2

The Gospel and Sanctification. I Peter 1:3—5:11

    The Gospel of an Incorruptible Heritage (1:3-12)
    The Sanctification the Gospel Requires (1:13—2:10)
    Behavior Reflecting the Sanctified Life (2:11—3:12)
    Sanctification Under Fire: Persecution for Righteousness' Sake
    (3:13—5:11)

Closing Greetings. I Peter 5:12-14

COMMENTARY

SALUTATION

I Peter 1:1-2

In its salutation, the First Letter of Peter follows with some alterations the usual form of a Greek letter of the day. The usual form was, "So-and-so to So-and-so, greetings." Paul had adopted this pattern but added certain phrases by way of description of himself as the writer and of the church addressed. These additions in some cases were quite extensive (see Rom. 1:1-7; I Cor. 1:1-3; Gal. 1:1-5). It had become Paul's habit to include, particularly in his description of the church addressed, certain items which suggested the content of the letter to follow. Paul had also expanded the usual term, "Greetings," into a benediction, thereby giving it a distinctively Christian flavor. It seems certain that the salutation of First Peter is definitely patterned after that employed by Paul.

The writer describes himself as "Peter, an apostle of Jesus Christ." There can be no doubt that the original disciple of Jesus of that name is intended. His Aramaic name was originally Simon Bar-Jona, but Jesus renamed him "Rock" (in Aramaic *Kepha,* in Greek *Petros;* see Matt. 16:17-18; John 1:41-42). It would be natural of course for Peter, in addressing churches in the Greek-speaking world, to employ his Greek name. The designation of himself as "an apostle of Jesus Christ" indicates the authority by which he writes.

The Christians or churches addressed are described by the author as the elect ("chosen") "exiles of the Dispersion in Pontus, Galatia, Cappadocia, Asia, and Bithynia" (vs. 1). The adjective "elect" or "chosen" is a New Testament description of Christians generally (Titus 1:1; see Eph. 1:4). The term was applied in the Old Testament to the Chosen People (see Ps. 105:6, 43; Isa. 45:4). "Exiles" (or "sojourners") is a term which lays stress upon the transitoriness of one's existence in a particular locality. It is intended to express the same thought as that in Hebrews 11:8-16 relative to Abraham and his descendants during their dwelling in the land of Canaan. This was merely a transitory existence, inasmuch as Abraham looked for the eternal city which

God had prepared for him. In consequence he and his descendants thought of themselves as "strangers and exiles on the earth" (Heb. 11:13). "Dispersion" originally indicated the Jews living outside Palestine (John 7:35; see also James 1:1). James and Peter in applying this term to the Christian Church were merely following the common custom of adopting terminology which originally referred to Israel and Judaism and of refurbishing it for Christian ends. The churches addressed probably include those to be found throughout Asia Minor north of the Taurus Mountains (see Introduction).

Verse 2 provides us with a good example—of which there are a number in the Epistles (II Cor. 13:14; Eph. 4:4-6)—of the type of passage out of which the later Trinitarian formula of the Church arose. "Destined by God the Father" is literally in the Greek, "according to the foreknowledge of God the Father." However, the participle "destined" gives the sense of the Semitic idiom lying behind the Greek; for in the Hebrew "to foreknow" often meant "to determine," "to decide," or "to predestine" (Amos 3:2; and see Rom. 8:29; 11:2). "Sanctified by the Spirit" is a phrase suggestive of the central teaching of the letter as a whole, which is to the effect that the Christian way is one of holiness or sanctification like to that of God (1:15-16). The work of both the Father and the Spirit is said to be for the purpose of the readers' "obedience to Jesus Christ" and their "sprinkling with his blood." These phrases also suggest major themes of the letter. In verse 14 obedience is set in contrast to "the passions of your former ignorance," and in verse 22 this obedience is further related to the subject of purification or sanctification and is defined as "obedience to the truth." Sprinkling with blood is a phrase suggestive of the worship in Tabernacle and Temple. Like the Letter to the Hebrews, the thought of First Peter moves in a circle of ideas suggested by that worship (see vs. 19 and Heb. 9:13, 19, 21; 10: 22, 29; 12:24).

At this point in the usual salutation of a Greek letter it was customary merely to express "greetings" (see James 1:1). Paul had baptized this usual salutation by employing another form of the same Greek word-stem, the noun "grace," referring to the unmerited love of God conferred upon the sinner in the work of Jesus Christ. With this noun Paul had also habitually joined the Greek term for "peace"—the translation of the Hebrew word which was also used as a greeting. This "peace" is understood as that between God and man, achieved by God's redemptive activity on man's behalf (Isa. 57:19; Eph. 2:14, 17). Peter was obviously acquainted with Paul's custom and simply took over his formula.

THE GOSPEL AND SANCTIFICATION

I Peter 1:3—5:11

The Gospel of an Incorruptible Heritage (1:3-12)

Its Assurance Resting on God's Mercy and Power (1:3-5)

At this point in his letters it was customary for Paul to insert a prayer of thanksgiving (see Rom. 1:8; I Cor. 1:4). However, he altered this formula in two directions: in Galatians 1:6 he inserted an anathema directed against those who had quickly departed from the "grace of Christ"; and in II Corinthians 1:3 he substituted a doxology for the usual thanksgiving (see also Eph. 1:3). First Peter, it will be observed, follows the latter pattern, resembling Ephesians more than Second Corinthians. The literary style is that known in Greek literature as a "period"—that is, a long involved and exceedingly complex sentence, highly ornamented with descriptive phrases and subordinate clauses, intended to supply beauty of syntactical structure worthy of a highly complex theme.

It is rather generally held that the major portion of the letter (1:3—4:11) follows the catechetical or baptismal formula of instruction given to new converts to the Christian faith in the Early Church (see Introduction). Following the usual pattern of this formula, the present section (vss. 3-12), in the form of a doxology, presents us with a somewhat comprehensive doctrinal statement. The theme of this doctrinal statement is "the good news" or gospel (vs. 12) of "an inheritance which is imperishable, undefiled, and unfading, kept in heaven for you" (vs. 4). Or again, it is the good news of "a living hope through the resurrection of Jesus Christ from the dead" (vs. 3). Finally, it may be defined as the good news of "a salvation ready to be revealed in the last time" (vs. 5). As will be seen, all of these descriptions of the content of the gospel are oriented toward the future, even toward the eternal order at the end of history.

The "living hope" to which Peter makes reference is doubtless the same as the "hope of eternal life" in Titus 1:2. As in all New Testament thought, such hope of life comes to the Christian "through the resurrection of Jesus Christ from the dead" (vs. 3; I Cor. 15:12, 13, 21; and see also Acts 23:6; 24:15; Heb. 6:18-20). Peter, accordingly, like the other writers of the Early Church, makes the resurrection of Jesus Christ the cornerstone of the Christian faith. And as with Paul, who witnesses to the tradition of the Church from the beginning (I Cor. 15:1-11), the resurrection of Christ is a matter of experience to which Peter testifies, not an abstraction to be proved by logic. The suggestion that "we have been born anew" to this hope of life approaches most nearly to the thought and terminology of the Gospel of John (see John 3:3, 7). Behind the experience, including the resurrection of Christ himself and our birth to this "living hope," lies the "great mercy" of "the God and Father of our Lord Jesus Christ." From the beginning the Church believed that it was the Father who had raised Jesus Christ from the dead (Acts 2:24, 32; I Cor. 15:15).

Peter speaks of this hope of life as "an inheritance" (vs. 4), a word taken over from the Old Testament promise with regard to Canaan (Gen. 17:8) and employed in the New Testament to refer to the fulfillment of all the promises of God (Acts 20:32; Gal. 3:18; Eph. 1:14, 18; 5:5; Heb. 9:15). The adjectives "imperishable," "undefiled," and "unfading" applied to this "inheritance" enhance the idea of its eternal value; together they are the equivalent of the expression that it is "kept in heaven" for the Christian. But if the "mercy" of God is behind the Christian's eternal hope, it is God's "power" which guarantees the safeguarding of both the Christian and his inheritance (vs. 5). "Salvation" is the third of the trilogy of words ("hope," "inheritance," "salvation") which together represent the redemption to be received by the Christian. This salvation is not in its entirety a present possession; the believer is "guarded through faith" for its final reception. And yet for Peter "the last time" has already arrived, as in verse 20 he commits himself to the idea that Christ has already been "made manifest at the end of the times" (see also 4:7).

Trial of Our Faith in It (1:6-9)

In the previous section Peter remarks that "faith" is the response which man must make to the salvation proffered by God (vs. 5). The present passage analyzes the circumstances under which the Christian must express this response of faith, the circumstances of a realistic world in which the Christian is called upon "to suffer various trials" (vs. 6). These "trials" are very real and are calculated to test "the genuineness of . . . faith," even as "gold . . . is tested by fire" (vs. 7). There is no indication that the "trials" intended are of any special severity; indeed, Peter suggests in verse 6 that they are only a possibility with which the Christian has to reckon. In any case "various trials" are a commonplace in Christian experience, as is also the paradox that in the midst of trial and tribulation Christians may "rejoice."

The Christian's joy is the product of his realization of the "salvation" which he has already begun to experience and to whose consummation he looks forward (vss. 3-5). Jesus had long since comforted his disciples with the thought that joy in the midst of persecution was not only possible for the Christian but also placed him in the category of the prophets of old time who had had a similar experience (Matt. 5:11-12). Paul had testified to his having experienced joy in the midst of suffering (Col. 1:24; see also Rom. 5:3-5; II Cor. 6:10). Moreover, the "little while" (vs. 6) reminds us of the similar teaching in Hebrews 10: 32-39 and 12:3-11.

It is a psychologically well-authenticated fact, and one attested by Christian experience, that joy may thus be experienced in the midst of suffering, provided the sufferer realizes at the time the larger goal to be attained as the product of the suffering. In the present instance this goal is stated to be both proximate and more remote. The proximate or near goal is the testing of "the genuineness" of the "faith" of Peter's readers (vs. 7); the remote object of this testing is that these Christians' faith "may redound to praise and glory and honor at the revelation of Jesus Christ." Probably "praise and glory and honor" here refer to one thing, namely, Christ's pleasure at and acceptance of the believer's faith as the sole condition of his salvation. The event intended in the expression "the revelation of Jesus Christ" is, of course, the final coming and the Judgment at the end of the age.

Peter now dwells on the paradoxical nature of his readers' faith in Christ (vss. 8-9). They have never "seen him," and yet they "love him," and though they "do not now see him," they "believe in him and rejoice with unutterable and exalted joy." Such is the paradoxical nature of the love and faith of Christians at all times. For they are called upon to live in a world of nature which is apprehended by the five senses. And yet it is both their duty and their privilege to employ the sixth sense of "faith" in apprehending him who is invisible (see John 20:29; I Cor. 13:12; Heb. 11:27). The outcome of such faith is now said to be "the salvation of your souls" (vs. 9), which is the practical equivalent of the "praise and glory and honor" which we have already noted (vs. 7).

This Gospel Prophesied of Old (1:10-12)

Peter brings the long Greek "period" to a close with a comprehensive reference to the Hebrew prophets' knowledge of and witness to the Christian's salvation. They "inquired," he says, with regard to the nature of the "salvation" itself, the "person" by whom it was to be achieved, and the "time" when this would occur (vss. 10-11). He remarks almost incidentally that such salvation was to be the product of "the grace" of God and that the source of the revelation which came to the prophets was "the Spirit of Christ within them." And he speaks of their "predicting the sufferings of Christ and the subsequent glory" which should follow them. In these two verses—packed as they are in every word and phrase with deep doctrinal content—we can feel Peter's assurance, perhaps reflecting the knowledge that he was simply repeating what was already known to his Christian readers through tradition. For it is beyond dispute that the Christian Church from the beginning found in the Old Testament Scriptures, and particularly in their prophetic sections, unmistakable reference to Jesus Christ and the salvation which he would accomplish in the providence of God and in his own good time (see Mark 14:21, 27; Luke 24:44-47; John 2:17; 12:14-16; Acts 2:15-36).

The continuity between the Old Covenant and the New is further elaborated in verse 12. Here it is explicitly stated that "the things" with which the prophets dealt formed the content of "the good news" which was preached later on to the Christians of Peter's generation. Moreover, just as these things were "indicated by the Spirit of Christ" to the prophets, so they were "announced" by Christian evangelists, "through the Holy Spirit sent from heaven" to Peter's readers!

Two points stand out with unmistakable clarity in this passage: First, the fact that it owes much to the description of the Suffering

Servant in Second Isaiah. Both Jesus Christ himself and the Church which he established interpreted his own sufferings in terms of those of this Suffering Servant (compare Luke 22:37 with Isa. 53:12; Acts 8:32-33 with Isa. 53:7-8; Heb. 9:28 with Isa. 53: 12). Second, the phraseology of the passage contains clear similarity to that in the Letter to the Hebrews. Thus, the fact that "the things" constituting the "good news" were known and proclaimed by the Old Testament prophetic characters is the theme of Hebrews, chapters 3 and 4 (see particularly 4:1-7). Similarly, the idea that these prophetic figures were "serving not themselves but you" has its certain counterpart in Hebrews 11:39-40, while the reference to "angels" and their attachment to the gospel and its proclamation is found in Hebrews 1:14 (see also Heb. 2:16). There may even be an intended contrast between the fact that "angels long to look" into the gospel and its nature (vs. 12) and the tradition held by Hellenistic-Jewish Christians that the Law had been "declared by angels" (Heb. 2:2; see also Acts 7:53; Gal. 3:19).

The Sanctification the Gospel Requires (1:13—2:10)

A Holy Life—God's Example and the Christian's Hope (1:13-17)

From this point forward to 5:11 Peter's style is largely hortatory. Here and there are interspersed sections of a purely doctrinal nature, but generally speaking doctrine forms an integral part of the exhortation itself. The introductory word "therefore" with which this section opens refers to the doctrinal passage which precedes. Exhortation to holy living is based upon the theology at which we have been looking. More specifically, such living may be said to be the joint product of the grace of God the Father (vss. 3, 10), the redemptive work of Christ (vss. 3, 7, 11), and the indwelling of the Holy Spirit (vss. 2, 11, 12).

Following the pattern of the catechetical instruction given by the Early Church to its new converts, at this point Peter begins to lay stress upon the necessity of the holy life for the Christian. He sets it against the background of the pagan vices of the day and represents the Christian hope as its motive. We have already seen that he has set forth the "hope" of "the grace that is coming to you at the revelation of Jesus Christ" (vs. 13) as a principal theme for his readers' consideration (vss. 3,10-12). Neither here

nor elsewhere in the letter is Peter afraid of repetition, doubtless
using it—and quite properly so—as a pedagogical device. As before, therefore, we note that the "hope" is an eschatological one and
is not as yet entirely fulfilled in the experience of the Christian (see
vs. 5). Peter's suggestion to his readers in the words "gird up your
minds, be sober" is nearly identical with Paul's in Ephesians 6:14
("having girded your loins with truth"), and both are reminiscent of Isaiah's description of "the branch" of Jesse, of whom he
says that "righteousness shall be the girdle of his waist, and
faithfulness the girdle of his loins" (Isa. 11:5). All of these expressions reflect, of course, the oriental mode of dress with its
important cummerbund which forms the major support for the entire ensemble.

Like Paul in Acts 17:30, Peter thinks of the pre-Christian life
of his readers as one characterized by "ignorance" (vs. 14). Such
ignorance is found in the Jew as well as in the Greek (see Rom.
7:7), in both being essentially an ignorance of God's will for
man's life which expresses itself in giving way to "passions" (see
2:11; 4:2; Gal. 5:16-24). On the contrary, the "obedient" Christian is called upon to be "holy . . . in all . . . [his] conduct" (vs.
15), and this for the reason that God has made man in his image
and therefore to be holy as God himself is holy (vs. 16; see Lev.
19:2). The verse from Leviticus quoted here makes God himself
the pattern for man, who is in all his ways to mirror the likeness of
this "holy" God. For a somewhat similar Christian use of this
imagery see II Corinthians 3:17-18. Peter reminds his readers
that God is not only "Father" but is also one "who judges each
one impartially according to his deeds" (vs. 17). "Fear" of this
holy God is accordingly not without its place in Christian exper
ience, or, as Peter remarks, "throughout the time of your exile,"
that is, of one's absence from the heavenly order which is the
Christian's home (see vs. 1).

A Holy Life—Achieved by Christ's Death and Resurrection (1:18-21)

Peter, however, has no illusions about the power of Christians
to emulate the high pattern set for them by the holy God. Indeed,
he affirms that our "faith and hope are in God" alone (vs. 21).
He has already said that this holy God is none other than "the God
and Father of our Lord Jesus Christ" (vs. 3). Accordingly, "before the foundation of the world" God had set his mind to working

out a plan of salvation whereby men might be "ransomed from the futile ways inherited" from the past (vss. 18, 20). This method of salvation involved the sending of Christ into the world that he might die, be "raised" again "from the dead," and be glorified "for your sake" (vss. 19-21).

Peter does not work out in detail for us the method whereby the Christian's salvation to a holy life is achieved through the death and resurrection of Jesus Christ. In language taken from the slave market on the one hand, and the worship of the altar on the other, he merely suggests that Christ's death has purchased us for God (vss. 18-19). The word "ransomed" or "redeemed" (Isa. 52:3) is one reminiscent of the slave market (Rom. 3:24; I Cor. 6:20; 7:23), and to the Jew always brought to mind the period of bondage in Egypt (Acts 7:30-37). In the Christian's case the metaphor was used for his deliverance from "the futile ways inherited from . . . [his] fathers." But the ransom price is stated in sacrificial terms as having been constituted by "the precious blood of Christ, like that of a lamb without blemish or spot" (vs. 19; see Exod. 12:5; Lev. 9:3). Peter sees this work of Christ in the perspective of eternity, from which "he was destined," that is, predetermined, by God for the task of redemption which he fulfilled (see also II Cor. 5:19). Like Paul, Peter sees God as the creative agent in the resurrection of Christ; for it was God "who raised him from the dead and gave him glory" (vs. 21; see I Cor. 15:20-28).

Peter's declaration that Jesus Christ "was made manifest at the end of the times for your sake" (vs. 20) is indicative of the chronology with which he is working. There can be no doubt that whereas in verses 3, 7, and 13, as elsewhere in the letter, the coming of Christ at the end of history is in mind, in verse 20 the Incarnation is equally before the mind of the writer. Accordingly, it is clear that for him "the end" includes the period of history from the Incarnation forward, and that the entire period of Church history may be identified with "the last times." In this respect Peter is in accord with the other New Testament writers who expressed themselves on the subject (see Acts 2:16-21; I Cor. 10:11; Heb. 1:2; I John 2:18).

A Holy Life—Generated by the Word (1:22—2:3)

In saying that the Christian's "confidence" is "in God" (vs. 21), or in his "great mercy" (vs. 3) or "grace" (vss. 10, 13), Peter has presented to his readers the ultimate source of their salvation. He now indicates the means or instrument which God has employed to accomplish his will in this matter. This instrument is "the living and abiding word of God" (vs. 23) or "the good news" (vs. 25), that is to say, the gospel "which was preached" to these Christians and which resulted in their rebirth (vs. 23; see also 2:2).

In this doctrine of the new birth Peter shows affinity with several other New Testament writers. The teaching is essentially the same as that at John 3:1-10. But the sowing of the "word of God" which results in regeneration is also the theme of the parable of the Sower (Matt. 13:1-9, 18-23). And the same series of ideas (living word, sowing, rebirth) with natural variations in the use of terminology is found also abundantly in both Paul (I Cor. 1:18-25; 2:1-5; Eph. 1:13; Col. 1:5, 25; 3:16) and Hebrews (4:2, 12; 13:7).

The response to this "word of God" or "good news" is that "obedience to the truth" which results in purification (vs. 22). Peter nowhere else in the letter uses the word "truth," but in 1:2 he speaks of "obedience to Jesus Christ" and in 2:8 of those who "disobey the word." We may put together the three passages and through their conjoint testimony discover that the "obedience" which he has in mind is that relating to Jesus Christ, or alternatively to the "truth," or to the "word." So that whether one say "word," "gospel," "good news," "truth," or "Jesus Christ," it would seem obvious that for Peter one is saying essentially the same thing. For him Jesus Christ is the content of the word, of the truth, of the gospel message. And there is considerable evidence in the New Testament that for the Early Church such equations were generally acceptable (Eph. 1:13; Col. 1:5, 25). According to Acts 15:9, Peter had maintained that the Holy Spirit had "cleansed their [the Gentiles'] hearts by faith." And though the Greek is not identical, the meaning is essentially the same as "having purified your souls," which Peter here says is the result of "obedience to the truth" (1:22).

The result of this rebirth and obedience or purification is "sincere love of the brethren" (vs. 22), or the putting away of "all malice and all guile and insincerity and envy and all slander" (2:1). And so the Christian trilogy of faith, hope, and love is complete (see vss. 3, 9, 13 above for "faith" and "hope"; and I Cor. 13:13; Heb. 10:39; 11:1; 13:1).

Peter's readers were evidently quite recent converts, as he styles them "newborn babes" (2:2), an expression which in the Greek refers to the youngest type of infant, a babe in arms (see Luke 2:12, 16; 18:15; Acts 7:19). The phrase is nowhere else used in the New Testament in this spiritualized sense regarding converts, though a somewhat similar one is used of those who are mere "babes in Christ" in I Corinthians 3:1-2 and Hebrews 5:12-14. The phraseology, indeed, of verses 2 and 3 is quite similar to that in Hebrews 5:12—6:8. There is, however, a distinct difference in that Hebrews blames its readers for not having gone on to maturity, in view of the considerable lapse of time since their conversion (see 5:12), whereas Peter expects his "newborn babes" to continue to long for the "spiritual milk" which apparently they still require.

A Holy Life—Incarnated in the Church (2:4-10)

This passage contains one of the most beautiful as well as most comprehensive descriptions of the Christian Church to be found in the New Testament. It has been suggested that it is derived from the stanzas of a Christian hymn which Peter took over and incorporated in his letter. In general it forms a Christian interpretation of three passages from the Old Testament—Isaiah 28:16 (vs. 6); Psalm 118:22 (vs. 7); and Isaiah 8:14-15 (vs. 8). Other Old Testament passages, however, are brought into use and phrases from them adopted, as, for instance, Exodus 19:6 in verse 9; Isaiah 43:20-21 in the same verse; and Hosea 1:6, 9 and 2:23 in verse 10. Numerous phrases in the passage also link it to certain sayings of Jesus in the Gospels, to the Letters of Paul, the Letter to the Hebrews, and the Book of Revelation. Whether Peter constructed this section himself or inherited it in the tradition of the Church, its author has done a masterly piece of work in describing the Christian Church—its origin, its nature, and its function.

The main teaching of the passage is to the effect that the Christian Church is "a spiritual house" (vs. 5; see Heb. 3:6), that is, a house of worship whose cornerstone is the "living stone," Jesus Christ himself (vs. 4; see Eph. 2:20). Such a Church is constituted itself of "living stones" (vs. 5; see Eph. 2:21-22; 4:15-16). Or, to change the metaphor, since the "spiritual house" in question is one for the worship of God, its household may be thought of as "a holy priesthood, to offer spiritual sacrifices" (vs. 5)—sacrifices "acceptable to God through Jesus Christ," presumably because, as

Peter has already indicated, it is through the work of Christ that the Church is in the process of being saved (1:18-21). Or, once again slightly changing the metaphor, this "spiritual house" is actually "a chosen race, a royal priesthood, a holy nation, God's own people" (vs. 9), a passage in which the phrases quoted are largely from Exodus 19 and 23 and from Isaiah 43, as suggested above. Or, once again changing the metaphor and employing Hosea 1 and 2, the Christian household of faith may be described as made up of those who "once . . . were no people but now . . . are God's people; once . . . had not received mercy but now . . . have received mercy" (vs. 10).

The center about which this entire description of the Church revolves is the quotation in verse 7 from Psalm 118:22, a passage cited elsewhere in the New Testament. According to the Gospel writers, Jesus himself employed it with regard to himself (Matt. 21:42; Mark 12:10-11; Luke 20:17). Peter employs the verse in a sermon (Acts 4:11) as well as in the present passage, and the contiguous verses of the Psalm are used by other New Testament writers. Peter, then, or the traditional hymn which he inserts in his letter, attached to this verse from the Psalm two verses from Isaiah (28:16 and 8:14-15) which also speak of "a stone" which was "chosen and precious" in the sight of God but calculated to "make men stumble" who did not accept Jesus Christ. (Paul also employs the same passages and circle of ideas in Romans 9:25-33, as well as the ideas from Hosea 1 and 2 found in verse 10.)

Implicit in the passage as a whole is the idea that Jesus Christ is the great High Priest over God's "spiritual house," although Peter neither here nor elsewhere applies this term to him; and that the Church as a whole, as he says specifically, is under Christ "a holy priesthood" or "a royal priesthood," performing "spiritual sacrifices" (vs. 5) which are acceptable to God, even as Christ's sacrifice was (see also Col. 1:24; Heb. 9:13-14; Rev. 1:6; 5:10; 20:6).

This idea of Jesus Christ as High Priest and of Christians as priests, and of the personal sacrifices which both render in their worship to God, is akin to the thought of Hebrews. It is striking that in the one (Hebrews) Jesus Christ is called "high priest" (6:20; 9:11; 10:21), though his followers are never called "a priesthood," whereas in First Peter the situation is exactly reversed. His followers, as we have just seen, are called "a holy priesthood" (vs. 5) and "a royal priesthood" (vs. 9), but Peter

never speaks of Jesus as "high priest." But perhaps the most striking similarity between this passage and Hebrews is found in their
joint teaching that the sin which characterizes those who "stumble"
upon the stone or rock which is Jesus Christ, is that "they disobey
the word" (vs. 8; see Heb. 3:18).

Three further points remain to be noted. First, the idea that
Jesus was "rejected by men but in God's sight chosen and precious"
(vs. 4) is similar in its teaching to that found in Peter's sermon at
Pentecost in Acts 2:22-36, and likewise the reference to the "wonderful deeds of him who called you" (vs. 9) is akin in meaning
to the "mighty works and wonders and signs which God did"
through "Jesus of Nazareth, a man attested to you by God" in
Acts 2:22. Second, that the Christian readers of the letter have
been called "out of darkness into his [God's] marvelous light"
(vs. 9) is a common New Testament way of speaking of those
who are converted from paganism to the true faith (see Acts
26:18; Col. 1:13-14). The idea no doubt derives from such passages as Isaiah 42:6-7 and 16 in which the work of the Servant
of the Lord is under consideration. Finally, the idea that the
readers once were "no people" and are now "God's people," that
they had at one time "not received mercy" but now "have received
mercy" (vs. 10), enshrines the very heart of the Christian gospel
as that is prefigured in the emblematic prophecy uttered by Hosea
with regard to his adulterous wife (Hosea 1 and 2).

Behavior Reflecting the Sanctified Life (2:11—3:12)

Good Conduct Among Non-Christians (2:11-12)

The quotation from the hymn (if such it be) inserted in verses
4-10 above has served to establish the fact that the Christian community is the true people of God. Peter now turns, accordingly,
to a discussion of the behavior which should characterize that
people, particularly "among the Gentiles" (vs. 12). The word
here translated "Gentiles" both in the Greek and in the Hebrew
lying behind it actually means "nations," and Peter in employing
it is simply following the common New Testament practice (see
Rom. 2:14; I Cor. 1:23), thereby in a formal manner perpetuat-
ing the Jewish distinction between the people of God on the one
hand and the nations of the world on the other. It is, however, *only*
in a formal sense that the Christian Church speaks of itself as "a

chosen race" and "a holy nation" (vs. 9), as though it were, so to speak, a "third race" and thus distinct from both Jews and Gentiles. Actually, of course, the Christian community is composed of people of every race and nation without distinction. That this is Peter's view is evidenced by his employing the terms "aliens and exiles" (vs. 11; see 1:1) to describe the Christian community, a mode of expression found also in Hebrews 11:13.

The "good conduct" which Christians are to practice includes abstaining from "the passions of the flesh that wage war against . . . [the] soul" (vs. 11). The exact Greek of this phrase is not found elsewhere in the New Testament, its nearest equivalents being in Galatians 5:16-17, 24; Ephesians 2:3; II Peter 2:18; I John 2:16. In the expression "flesh" stands, not for the physical constitution of man as such, but rather for fallen human nature, that is, for man's entire person under the dominion of sin. And the thought that man's "flesh" in this sense is dominated by evil passions or desires which are contrary to God's will for his life is a rather common thought among the New Testament writers (see Rom. 7:7-25; 13:14; I Thess. 4:5; James 1:14-15; Jude 16 and 18). The old enemy of the fleshly passions remains alive to the very end and in consequence the Christian must never sleep.

The suggestion in verse 12 that Gentiles through the "good conduct" of Peter's readers should be led to "see . . . [their] good deeds and glorify God" is reminiscent of Jesus' saying in Matthew 5:16. As Paul remarks in Ephesians 2:10, the reason for glorifying God in this connection is the fact that he is himself the author of the good works of Christians, an idea which, as we have already seen, Peter has acknowledged (see 1:21, 22-25). The "day of visitation" referred to is that indicated in Isaiah 10:3 (Greek translation) and may be taken to mean generally the Day of Judgment.

The Christian's Obedience to Constituted Authority (2:13-17)

We are now to look in detail at the nature of the "good conduct among the Gentiles" which Peter pleads with his readers to maintain (vs. 12). This code of social ethics for the Christian has its nearest parallels in Paul (Rom. 13:1-7; Eph. 5:21—6:9; Col. 3:12 —4:1; I Tim. 2:1-15; 6:1-2; Titus 2:1—3:2). Some mention of it is also found in James 4:6-10. But Peter's comprehensive statement in verse 13 that the Christian is to "be subject for the Lord's sake to every human institution" has no exact parallel for breadth elsewhere in the Epistles. The code is obviously one of "submission" (vss. 13, 18; 3:1) or of subordination. As Peter sees it, this principle is utterly universal and includes "every human institution," that is, every element in the social order. Moreover, such subordination is "for the Lord's sake," an idea already implied in verse 12 in the injunction to "good deeds" with a view to the Gentiles' glorifying God.

Christians then are in a very real sense to know two masters —God and man. The origin of such teaching may well be the Church's Lord himself. For when confronted with the problem of the Christian's attitude toward the state he remarked, "Render to Caesar the things that are Caesar's, and to God the things that are God's" (Mark 12:17). By implication this means that the Christian is to realize that he is not only a citizen of heaven but as an "alien" and "exile" in the world he is also a citizen of the state and therefore subject to "every human institution." That, however, the Christian is to consider both God and the social order his master *on equal terms* is neither the teaching of Jesus (Matt. 6:24) nor that of the succeeding Church (Acts 4:19-20).

As the first and highest of the human institutions to which Peter refers, stands, of course, the state. In the context in which Peter was writing the state was represented by "the emperor as supreme" (vs. 13), and by the "governors" of the various imperial and senatorial provinces (vs. 14). Peter obviously sees in the Roman Empire a system of law and order of which it may justly be said that the aim is "to punish those who do wrong and to praise those who do right." And in this judgment he was undoubtedly right, even as was also Paul (Rom. 13:3-4). Like Paul also, Peter holds that such submission to the state is "God's will" for the Christian (vs. 15), and that in his performance of his civic duty the Christian may show himself an exemplary citizen of the state (Rom. 13:1-2, 5). Peter's attitude in this matter seems to suggest an early date for the letter, approximating that of Romans.

The principle underlying this submission to the state of which Peter speaks and other types of which he will speak in the succeeding verses (2:18—3:7) is that which Paul terms "the glorious liberty of the children of God" (Rom. 8:21; see also Gal. 5:13). Peter's statement of the principle approximates that in the Galatians passage just cited—"Live as free men, yet without using your freedom as a pretext for evil; but live as servants of God" (vs. 16). The freedom of the Christian is not to be confused with license or with anarchy, for as Paul elsewhere says, "God is not a God of confusion but of peace" (I Cor. 14:33). And Peter knew as Paul did that Christian freedom was not a freedom to sin but a freedom from sin and unto righteousness (Rom. 6:18). "As servants of God," therefore, Christians should be model citizens of the state.

In verse 17 we have perhaps the most comprehensive summary of the Christian faith and ethic to be found anywhere in the New Testament: "Honor all men. Love the brotherhood. Fear God. Honor the emperor." "Honor" is literally in the Greek "to set a value upon," "to estimate at true worth," "to respect." The same word is used with regard to the Christian's attitude toward all men, on the one hand, and toward the emperor, on the other. One may almost say that Peter's maxim amounts to this: "Treat every man as though he were a king." The tense of the verb, however, is significantly altered in the two cases. The command regarding the king literally means "go on honoring the emperor," as was suitable, since Christians, of course, as citizens of the state had always been doing just that. However, in the case of "all men" the tense employed may be translated "begin to honor all men" or, better still, "begin to treat every man as though he were a king"!

The fact that one is to "love the brotherhood" is not intended to militate against the law of love which Jesus laid down with regard to "the neighbor," meaning by the neighbor every man (Luke 10:25-37). For love of the neighbor is included in the command to "honor all men." But the Christian Church soon learned that within the brotherhood, centering about Christ as Lord of life, a new type of love had been born. This was a love involving not only respect for and utter commitment to one's neighbor's good, but also a unique affection and understanding born of a deep spiritual and moral experience in Christ. The command to "fear God" represents the typical Hebrew-Jewish attitude (Exod. 18:21; Lev. 19:14; Deut. 6:13), but it is also a worthy Christian motivation (see Acts 9:31; Rom. 3:18; II Cor. 5:11; 7:1; Eph. 5:21). Such "fear" in the Hebrew idiom represented an intimate understanding of God's right to the highest respect from man, inasmuch as he is the sovereign Lord in the moral order.

The Christian Servant's Submission to His Master (2:18-25)

Peter now turns from the state to the family as the recognized unit of the Church's life (see Eph. 5:21—6:9), and he takes as examples of the submissiveness which should be found in Chris-

tian family life the relation of servant to master and of wife to
husband, and the reverse. The term "be submissive" does not refer to slavish obedience. It assumes that one submits *himself* to
the authority of another or of any "human institution," including
the state, and that he does so of his own free will and with a view
to serving higher ends.

The higher ends which are to be served are indicated by certain phrases, such as: "for the Lord's sake" (vs. 13), "as servants
of God" (vs. 16), "mindful of God" (vs. 19), "God's approval"
(vs. 20), "because Christ also suffered for you, leaving you an
example, that you should follow in his steps" (vs. 21), "so that
some, though they do not obey the word, may be won without a
word by the behavior of their wives" (3:1).

In the present paragraph Peter does not have in mind Christian
"masters" exclusively; for those of whom he writes include the
"overbearing" (vs. 18), those because of whom the Christian servant ("houseboy," "slave") is "suffering unjustly" (vs. 19), those
of whom it may be said that, though Christian servants "do right,"
they nonetheless are called upon to "suffer for it" (vs. 20). Again,
as in verse 12 above, it is clear that these illustrations have in
mind "good conduct among the Gentiles." In point of fact, many
Christians in the earliest period of the Christian movement were
slaves, and their masters by and large were pagans. Philemon (of
Colossae?—see Col. 4:9), to whom Paul addressed his notable
little letter on behalf of Onesimus, was clearly an exception to this
rule (Philemon 16-20).

At this point Peter adds a series of verses (vss. 21-25) which
serve to mark out the position of the Christian slave in the whole
Christian movement as being at its very center and serving to define its very nature. For the function of the Christian slave, says
Peter, is in reality *a vocation* (vs. 21), wherein the Christian
slave is "called," by following the "example" of Christ in whose
"steps" he walks, to set forth the characteristic of humility which
was his Master's. In calling to mind Christ's "example," Peter employs the language relating to the Suffering Servant of the Lord
in Isaiah 53, as for example in verse 22—"he committed no sin;
no guile was found on his lips" (Isa. 53:9); in verse 24—"he himself bore our sins" (Isa. 53:4, 12); again in verse 24—"by his
wounds you have been healed" (Isa. 53:5); and in verse 25—"you
were straying like sheep" (Isa. 53:6). In addition, it has been
argued by some interpreters that in verse 24 we should read, not

"he himself bore our sins in his body on the tree," but, as in the margin, "carried up our sins in his body to the tree." If this translation is adopted, then possibly Peter has in mind the imagery of the "scapegoat" (Lev. 16:20-22), upon which the high priest on the Day of Atonement was supposed to load all the sins of the people. He then drove the "scapegoat" into the wilderness, and it thus literally carried away the people's sins. Peter may similarly be thinking of our Lord as carrying up the people's sins to the tree (or cross) and thus dismissing them, as they were dismissed in the wilderness by the "scapegoat."

Finally, in suggesting that Christian slaves "were straying like sheep" (vs. 25), "but have now returned to the Shepherd and Guardian of . . . [their] souls," Peter is calling upon a traditional characterization of his Master which probably goes back to Jesus himself (see Mark 6:34; 14:27; John 10:11-18; Heb. 13:20; Rev. 7:17). As the great Shepherd of the sheep Jesus takes the position which in prophetic thought has been accorded to God himself (see Ps. 23; Isa. 40:11). Nowhere else in the New Testament is the Greek word which is here translated "Guardian" applied to our Lord. The word generally refers to an overseer of the Christian community (Acts 20:28; Phil. 1:1; I Tim. 3:2; Titus 1:7), and later became the title of that official in the Christian Church called in English "the bishop." The use of the two terms here with reference to the Christian slave emphasizes the fact of the direct approach of the Christian, however humble, to the Lord himself, without mediation on the part of any other.

The Christian Wife's Subjection to Her Husband (3:1-6)

In asking that the wife "be submissive" (vs. 1), Peter is asking no more than he does of all Christians (male and female) with regard to duly constituted authority and "every human institution" (2:13). And as in the case of all "good conduct" expected of the Christian generally (2:12), the motivation suggested is an evangelistic one—so that "some . . . may be won without a word by the behavior of their wives." The sort of adornment to which Peter takes exception in verse 3, having to do as it does with "braiding of hair, decoration of gold, and wearing of robes," is quite similar to that suggested in I Timothy 2:9. Isaiah had long before expostulated against just this sort of finery (3:18-24), and John in Revelation in somewhat similar terms describes the "great harlot" Babylon (18:7, 16-17). In estimating the value of such teaching on Peter's part, we should bear in mind the fact that both rabbis and pagan moralists wrote in much the same vein, and that doubtless all four (prophet, Peter, rabbi, and moralist) had in mind the allurements practiced by profligate women in Jewish and pagan society.

The permanent value of Peter's teaching, as of the others cited, is to be found not in its negations but rather in its affirmations. For certainly no exception can be taken to his suggestion that the adornment of the Christian woman is to be that of "the hidden person of the heart with the imperishable jewel of a gentle and quiet spirit" (vs. 4). It is this "jewel" which God "who sees in secret" (Matt. 6:4, 6, 18) accounts "very precious."

Verse 6, alone in the New Testament, carries the implication that the wife is to "obey" as well as "be submissive" to her husband. It is to be noticed, however, that here the point refers to the fact that "Sarah obeyed Abraham, calling him lord." It is noteworthy that Peter proceeds, "And you are now her children," not if you also obey, but rather "if you do right and let nothing terrify you."

The Christian Husband in Relation to His Wife (3:7)

This single verse of instruction to the Christian husband carries a great weight of responsibility. There is nothing quite like it elsewhere in the New Testament, the nearest parallels being found in Ephesians 5:25-33 and Colossians 3:19 (see also I Cor. 7:1-7). In none of these passages are husbands enjoined to "be submissive" to their wives, as is the case in reverse. This is no doubt due to the fact that the submissiveness enjoined throughout from 2:13 onward and in the parallel passages cited is one which recognizes a duly constituted headship in each "human institution" (2:13). As in the state the emperor is head, so in the family it is to be acknowledged that the husband is head. Such headship in Christian circles is recognized as similar to that of Christ to his Church (Eph. 5:23-24), *a headship of love,* for as Paul says, "the husband is the head of the wife as Christ is the head of the church, his body, and is himself its Savior." Therefore, as he continues (Eph. 5:25), husbands are to love their wives "as Christ loved the church and gave himself up for her." Indeed, the husband's headship is limited to his being "the great lover" in the family, even as Christ is the great lover of his Church and is its Savior.

There can be no doubt that Peter is here dealing with the same circle of ideas as he suggests to husbands, "Live considerately with your wives, bestowing honor on the woman as the weaker sex" (vs. 7). In the Greek, "considerately" is literally "according to knowledge." That "the woman" is to be *honored* as "the weaker sex" implies the sort of paradoxical reversal of values which carries through the whole of the Christian ethic and is akin to the suggestion already made at 2:17, to the effect that all men are to be treated as though they were kings! It is as though Peter were saying that it is in the woman's weakness that her strength is to be found; not in physical prowess but in moral and spiritual (and no doubt also intellectual) qualities does her strength reside.

The ultimate reason for the Christian husband's so treating his wife is found in the fact that they are equally "heirs of the grace of life," and its aim is that their "prayers may not be hindered." Wife and husband are, in other words, on a spiritual par in the sight of God and, therefore, should be so in the sight of each other. Though the phraseology here is different, this exactly accords with the teaching of Jesus and of Paul regarding the moral and spiritual equality of men and women (Matt. 5:27-32; Mark 10:2-12; I Cor. 7).

Summary: Christian Behavior for All (3:8-12)

And now Peter summarizes for all his Christian readers the nature of the Christian ethic as it applies more particularly within the sphere of the brotherhood (vs. 8; see 2:17). In verse 8 he gives a comprehensive statement of Christian attitudes as these unfold from within and express themselves in outward action. It would seem that this verse should be read in reverse—the "humble mind," which realizes its own unworthiness in the sight of God and men, naturally expressing itself in "a tender heart" toward those who are in like fashion unworthy, such "a tender heart" finding room for "love of the brethren" as its normal expression, issuing in "sympathy," which in turn gives birth to "unity of spirit."

"Humble mind" represents an attitude which Peter considers basic to the Christian ethic, as is shown in the fact that in 5:5 he practically duplicates this comprehensive statement in 3:8. This "rock" man, whose spirit in the early days had been exceedingly hard to tame (Mark 8:31-33; John 13:8-9), had himself learned humility the hard way! But he had learned it.

At this point Peter quotes from Psalm 34:12-16 (vss. 10-12). This Psalm as a whole serves as a definition of the "poor man" (see Ps. 34:6), or the humble person, who finds that his help lies only in God, not in other men nor in self (see Matt. 5:3).

Stated both negatively and positively, then, the Christian is not to "return evil for evil or reviling for reviling" (see Matt. 5:39, 44; Luke 6:28; Rom. 12:14-21); rather he is to "bless" that he "may obtain a blessing" himself (vs. 9). Literally the Greek here reads "Bless . . . that you may inherit a blessing," which is much like the third beatitude—"Blessed are the meek, for they shall inherit the earth" (Matt. 5:5). And it is striking that this beatitude of Jesus is actually a quotation from Psalm 37:11 (a Psalm in which the "meek" man is defined), and that "poor" and "meek" in Hebrew are essentially the same word. It is, says Peter, to such a "humble mind" or to such meekness that the Christian is "called." Such humble-mindedness issues in blessedness both for the man himself and for all whom his life touches. Again, as we have seen previously (1:15; 2:9, 21), Peter thinks of all Christians as having received a vocation or "call" from God to lead the Christian life in its purity and fullness.

Sanctification Under Fire: Persecution for Righteousness' Sake (3:13—5:11)

Making Christ Lord (3:13-17)

Peter now begins to deal realistically with the situation in which his readers are found. And, as we shall discover at 4:12, this involves the presence of actual persecution. To be sure, Peter approaches this realistic situation somewhat cautiously, so much so that some have imagined that it was during the writing of the letter that he heard of the "fiery ordeal" which his readers were actually facing at the moment. This, it is said, explains the fact that not until 4:12 is actual mention made of present persecution. It would appear rather that, as indicated in the outline, the thought of "persecution for righteousness' sake" or of "sanctification under fire" is a major theme which Peter has had in mind from the beginning of the letter. It is because the Christian's "holy life," like that of the prophets before him and of his Lord, is under fire that Peter finds occasion to write to his readers at all. The section before us serves as an introduction to the final major division of the letter, in which this climactic note of suffering for righteousness' sake becomes the dominant theme.

As he opens this new theme Peter immediately strikes the highest note possible for the Christian who is faced with the necessity of undergoing persecution for his faith. Indeed, this note represents the only motivation that can find logical justification within the Christian philosophy of life. This motivation may be stated in either of two ways, both of them representing the very heart of the gospel message. These are—"suffer for righteousness' sake" (vs. 14), and "in your hearts reverence Christ as Lord" (vs. 15). These two motivations can be traced back to the teaching of Jesus himself (see Matt. 5:10-12; Mark 8:34-38). Indeed, the first part of verse 14 sounds like a quotation of the eighth Beatitude (Matt. 5:10). Similarly, the first part of verse 15 is without doubt Peter's version of the common Christian tradition which Paul voices in I Corinthians 12:3: "No one can say 'Jesus is Lord' except by the Holy Spirit."

It is perhaps suggestive of the dual character (Gentile and Jewish) of his Christian readers' backgrounds that Peter at this point employs in the Greek two words of an abstract sort to suggest the ideal for which Christian suffering is undertaken—"what is right" (vs. 13) and "righteousness" (vs. 14). The two terms, expressing respectively the Greek and Hebrew conceptions of the ideal for man, are intended to stand for the same thing and both together represent the holy life which all along Peter has been setting forth as the Christian ideal. The Christian is not to allow any secular phenomenon to "terrify" (vs. 6) him or to fear lest it may "harm" (vs. 13) him. Those who are terrified and fear the harm which the world can do to them usually indulge in "reviling" (vs. 9), as our modern psychology now agrees. Neither the inner fear nor the outward expression of returning "evil for evil" and "reviling for reviling" are to be the Christian's attitude.

Peter has already drawn upon Isaiah 8:14-15—a messianic passage—for his reference to "a stone that will make men stumble, a rock that will make them fall" (2:8). He now calls upon verses 12-13 of the same chapter in Isaiah as he says with regard to what the world can do to the Christian: "Have no fear of them, nor be troubled, but in your hearts reverence Christ as Lord" (vss. 14-15).

The Christian then is always to be "prepared to make a defense to any one who calls . . . [him] to account for the hope that is in

... [him]" (vs. 15). As we have already observed (1:3, 13), this is the eschatological "hope" relating to the Final Coming, as the passages cited indicate. It is by no means an uncertain or weak element of the Christian faith; rather, it is "a sure and steadfast anchor of the soul," since it rests upon the saving activity of the incarnate Christ (see Heb. 6:19-20 and the comment on I Peter 4:18-22). The Christian's "defense," however, is always to be "with gentleness [meekness] and reverence," not with arrogant self-assertiveness (vs. 15; see Matt. 5:5; II Cor. 10:1; Gal. 6:1).

The proper armor of the Christian who is reviled by the secular world is "good behavior in Christ" (vs. 16), for there is nothing short of this which will make it possible for the Christian to keep his "conscience clear" (literally, "a good conscience"; see Acts 23:1; I Tim. 1:5, 19; II Tim. 1:3; Heb. 13:18; and I Peter 3:21). As before at 2:15, behind the Christian's conscience stands "God's will" (vs. 17). That "will" stands as the Lord of the conscience; it alone is the standard for what is "the good" or "righteousness."

Example of Christ's Suffering and Resurrection (3:18-22)

This section contains what is probably the most difficult problem of interpretation in the entire letter. The general teaching of the section, however, is clear enough. Employing some of the same terminology as at 2:21-25 (a passage which in turn employs the phraseology of Isaiah 53 relating to the Suffering Servant), Peter points out that Jesus Christ is at once Savior of and example to Christians, inasmuch as he "died for sins once for all, the righteous for the unrighteous, that he might bring us to God" (vs. 18). This death was followed by "the resurrection of Jesus Christ, who has gone into heaven and is at the right hand of God" (vss. 21-22). The passage has numerous other New Testament parallels (for example, Acts 2:22-36; Rom. 6:1-11; Phil. 2:5-11; Heb. 2:10-18).

Possibly in verse 18, instead of "died," we should read "suffered" (see margin). The passage would then parallel 2:21 and would correspond to the phraseology in 3:14 immediately above. This reading, if correct, has the advantage of stating explicitly that Christ's sufferings are to be an example to us, who like him are called upon to "suffer" and thus fulfill "God's will" for our lives (vs. 17), even as Christ was himself doing in dying for our sins (2:20-21). Peter's suggestion that Christ died "that he might bring us to God" approximates the thought of Paul (Rom. 5:2; Eph. 2:17-18; 3:12), and that of the author of Hebrews (4:16;

7:25; 10:1, 22). Such phraseology suggests that the end and aim of the Christian faith is to restore that fellowship with God on man's part which was broken by man's rebellion in the Garden of Eden (Gen. 3:22-24).

Jesus is able thus to "bring us to God" (vs. 18), because his death was followed by resurrection and ascension to "the right hand of God" (vss. 21-22), where "angels, authorities, and powers" have become "subject to him." This again is the same teaching as that found in the passages cited above—Jesus' death is followed by resurrection, a resurrection which implies his acceptance by God and his assumption of God's power. Needless to say, the assumption of such power on Jesus' part results in the salvation of the people for whom he died.

It is obvious from the passage that induction into Christ by "baptism" (vs. 21) is assumed by Peter as the visible and formal method through which the salvation offered in Christ's death and resurrection is applied to the believer. It is clear, too, that for him such baptism is not to be conceived in any mechanical sense (the thought no doubt intended in the words "not as a removal of dirt from the body"); rather it is to be understood as "an appeal to God for a clear conscience," that is, as a rite signifying an inner or spiritual change in the life of the believer. Such teaching with regard to the significance of baptism as the initial sacrament of the Christian faith is also to be illustrated elsewhere in the New Testament (Acts 2:38; 8:16, 36-38; Rom. 6:4; Col. 2:12). It is only, therefore, in this deep spiritual sense that it may be said that baptism "now saves you." For this rite signifies that the believer has been inducted into Christ and has "put on Christ" (Gal. 3:27; see Rom. 6:4).

The portion of the passage which we have referred to as difficult of interpretation is that found between the phrases "being put to death" and "saved through water" (vss. 18-20). Various suggestions for interpretation have been made, as follows: (1) it is suggested that verses 18-22 constitute a baptismal hymn to Christ, and that Peter incorporated this well-known hymn into the body of his letter as he had already done previously at 2:4-10 with a Christian hymn in praise of the Christian Church; (2) in the Greek, the introductory words in verse 19 ("in which he") may with a slight change be made to read rather "Enoch," or perhaps better "in which also Enoch," and it is therefore suggested that Peter here is referring, not to something which Jesus did in the spirit, but rather to the work of the patriarch Enoch (see Gen. 5:21-24), as this is reported in the apocryphal work of First Enoch (ch. 6); (3) the alternative possibility is suggested that these words should read "in which Noah" on the basis of the fact that the incident referred to occurred "in the days of Noah" (vs. 20); (4) the usual interpretation is that Peter is referring to what occurred in our Lord's experience between his death and resurrection; namely, that after his "death in the flesh," but while still "alive in the spirit" (vs. 18), he took occasion to descend, as the Creed suggests, "into hell" or alternatively "into Hades or Sheol," that is, into the abode of the dead, and that he there "preached to the spirits in prison" (vs. 19); finally (5) the suggestion is made that it is the pre-existent Christ to whom Peter refers as "alive in the spirit" and who "in the days of Noah" had "preached to the spirits" through his servant Noah—spirits who were incarnate or living men in Noah's day but who had since become "spirits in prison," that is, in hell or Sheol, because they did not respond to the preaching of Christ through Noah.

All of these interpretations have, as may easily be seen, points to commend them, and all equally have others which may be cited against them. It is this which makes the passage so very difficult of interpretation. It may be remarked that there is no other passage in the New Testament quite like this one; those most nearly approximating to its teaching are Romans 10:5-7 and Ephesians 4:8-10. If we feel impelled by the evidence to adopt the more common interpretation outlined above under (4), then several observations may justifiably be made. First, it is to be noted that no doctrine of purgatory with attendant Masses for the dead, works of supererogation, and the like, intended to deliver "the spirits in prison" by mechanical means manipulated by an almighty church, can remotely be substantiated by the passage. Second, Peter introduced this difficult passage to indicate how "God's patience" extends not only to the living but also to the dead "spirits in prison," a view which, although differently expressed, is in line with the gracious character of God as outlined throughout the Old and New Testaments (see, for example, Rom. 5:15-21; I Cor. 15:22; I Tim. 2:3-4). Third, Peter must have had the subsidiary motive of drawing out an analogy to baptism (vs. 21), which he finds strangely enough in the salvation accorded by the "ark" to "eight persons," who "in the days of Noah . . . were saved through water" (vs. 20). To our minds the analogy may seem far-fetched, but parallels for such analogies may be found in the teachings of the rabbis of the period and even in the writing of the Apostle Paul, who finds an analogy to baptism in the experience of Israel at the Red Sea (I Cor. 10:2) and to the Lord's Supper in the Israelites' being sustained by "supernatural food" and "supernatural drink" during the period of the wilderness wandering (I Cor. 10:3-4). However we may interpret this difficult passage, we must agree that it lies on the periphery of Christian truth.

Sharing Christ's Sufferings and Sinlessness in the Flesh (4:1-11)

Having established the fact that it is the Christian's obligation to make Christ his Lord (3:15-17), and further having portrayed the example of suffering which this Lord has undergone "for sins" (3:18-22), in the present passage Peter unhesitatingly exhorts his readers to emulate the sufferings and sinlessness of their Lord. In enjoining this imitation of Christ, as before (2:12) Peter is conscious of the Gentile world surrounding the Christian community as an ocean of evil might surround an island of purity (vs. 3). His readers are to "let the time that is past suffice for doing what the Gentiles like to do." Their actions are not to be affected in any way when these Gentiles "are surprised that . . . [they] do not now join them in the same wild profligacy" in which they indulge themselves (vs. 4), although "abuse" is likely to result. Peter consoles his readers, moreover, with the thought that these Gentiles "will give account to him who is ready to judge the living and the dead" (vs. 5).

It is not suffering in general that Peter has in mind but, as the whole letter shows, it is suffering "for righteousness' sake" (3:14), the only Christian suffering which could legitimately be parallel to that of the Christian's Lord. One who has thus vicariously suffered in the flesh may be said to have "ceased from sin," or perhaps better, to have "done with sin." The form of the verb in the Greek suggests an active determination to cease from sin, illustrated in the willingness of the Christian to suffer vicariously for righteousness' sake. Moreover, this interpretation is borne out by the following verse, which declares that the purpose of the Christian to have done with sin is "so as to live for the rest of the time in the flesh no longer by human passions but by the will of God" (vs. 2). Peter is not saying, then, as some of the Jewish rabbis said, that suffering and death on the part of an individual achieved atonement from sin for him. On the contrary, he is saying, if we understand his thought, that suffering "for righteousness' sake" is an indication that one has determined once for all to come to grips with the problem of sin and to have done with it, living his life henceforward "by the will of God" (see Rom. 6:15-19).

There are a number of parallels in the New Testament to the Gentile sins of which Peter gives a catalogue in verse 3 (see Rom. 1:28-32; Gal. 5:19-21; Eph. 5:3-5; Col. 3:5-9; I Tim. 1:8-11; Rev. 21:8; 22:15). The references cited are only a selection of the more obvious passages cataloguing the current sins of the day. It need not startle us that Peter suggests that the Gentiles were "surprised" at Christians for their unwillingness to "join them in the same wild profligacy" (vs. 4). The high ethical standards set forth in the Scriptures had constantly to battle against the profligacy of the surrounding paganism, in which it was by no means obvious that religion and morals have any necessary relation the one to the other. And Peter as before (3:18) asserts that it was because pagans did not see this connection that "the gospel was preached even to the dead," that they might, so to speak, be given a "chance" to accept the truth. The same difficulty arises in connection with this saying in verse 6 as in 3:18-22. Whatever the expression "to the dead" both here and in the former passage may mean, it is at least clear that here Peter compares human judgment according to standards which are current on earth with the eternal life which is lived in the presence of God. And in the context of the passage as a whole, his meaning is that, whatever may be the standards employed for men's judgments in this life, his readers should remember that "the gospel" as preached—wherever this is done, whether to the living or the dead—proclaims a life "in the spirit" whose only possible norm or standard is the life of God.

In this passage Peter also presents a short résumé of the type of ethical living expected of the Christian in view of the imminence of the divine judgment. "The end of all things is at hand; therefore keep sane and sober for your prayers" (vs. 7). Such statements need not be pressed to mean that the author in question expected that the end of history was just around the corner. All that they need mean is that from the Incarnation forward the Christian Church is living in "the last time" (see 1:5). The certainty of judgment, however, is suggested as a motive for right living, and this same motivation is attributed in the New Testament to Jesus himself (Mark 13:32-37; see also I Thess. 5:1-11).

Peter sets certain Christian characteristics over against the "human passions" of Gentile living. The formula follows somewhat the pattern set by Paul in Galatians 5:16-24, in which he speaks on the one hand of the "works of the flesh" (vs. 19), and on the other, of the "fruit of the spirit" (vs. 22). And similarly, the "gift," of which Peter speaks as being the product of "God's varied grace" (vs. 10), reminds one of Paul's reference to the "varieties of gifts" which are given by "the Spirit" to the members of "the body of Christ" (I Cor. 12).

In suggesting that Christians should have "love for one another, since love covers a multitude of sins" (vs. 8), Peter may be using a well-known quotation from Proverbs 10:12 (see also James 5:20). Love is prepared to overlook, to forgive, to bear with, and so in a real sense to "cover" the sins of others (see I Cor. 13:7). "Hospitality" (vs. 9) among Christian brethren was a most desirable trait in a community almost isolated from its pagan neighbors (see Rom. 12:13; I Tim. 3:2; Titus 1:8; Heb. 13:2).

The motivation for such Christian living, as is expressed elsewhere in the New Testament in varied forms, is "in order that in everything God may be glorified through Jesus Christ" (vs. 11; see I Cor. 10:31). The present section, which follows the pattern of catechetical instruction, ends with a doxology: "To him belong glory and dominion for ever and ever. Amen" (vs. 11). It is almost identical with that found in Romans 16:27. It is also quite similar to the second-century addition to the Lord's Prayer (Matt. 6:13, see margin), an addition which is patterned after the doxology found in David's prayer in I Chronicles 29:11-13.

Sharing Christ's Sufferings and Glory (4:12-19)

Some have thought that at this point in the letter Peter learns for the first time that "the fiery ordeal" of persecution is being experienced by the Christians to whom he is writing (vs. 12). The Greek translated "which comes upon you" may be rendered so as to refer to a present experience ("which *is presently* upon you"). But again, it lends itself also to the meaning "which *is about to come* upon you." In any case, Peter's point is threefold: first, whenever "fiery ordeal" of persecution comes upon the Christian he should understand that it is within the will of God and is intended to "prove" him (that is, to "put him to the test"); second, such testing is neither new nor strange; and third, the Christian should always be prepared to "rejoice" at sufferings which mean that he is being "reproached for the name of Christ" (vs. 14), or that he is suffering "as a Christian" (vs. 16). All three points are clearly made by Peter, no matter what the exact experience may be to which he refers in the phrase "the fiery ordeal."

The striking contrast between the two possible causes of suffering—on the one hand, "for the name of Christ" or "as a Christian," and on the other, "as a murderer, or a thief, or a wrongdoer, or a mischief-maker" (vs. 15)—brings before the mind of the reader the picture of Christ between the two thieves. These men apparently were not robbers of the ordinary type; presumably they were revolutionaries or extreme nationalists. And the words in verse 15 may very well describe just such political agitators.

There can be no doubt that the early group of followers about Jesus was at first strongly attracted to the idea of a nationalistic messiah, one who would deliver the Jews from the hands of their oppressors, the Romans (see Acts 1:6). Perhaps we should see in both Simon the Zealot and Judas Iscariot former members of this inner circle of revolutionaries. It is even possible that Peter's loss of faith in his Master and the movement for which he stood was due to his own concept of the nationalist movement and its nationalist messiah (see Matt. 26:58; Mark 14:26-31, 47-50; John 18:10-27). It would seem likely, then, that in the present passage Peter is concerned to point out to his Christian readers, whatever their background may be, that reproach "for the name of Christ" means something far more significant than suffering for a mere worldly or nationalistic messiah. For Jesus is not a mere nationalistic messiah but rather is God's Messiah, and to suffer for him is to "glorify God" (vs. 16) because "his glory" is God's glory, and to share his name and his reproach is to share "the spirit of glory and of God" (vs. 14).

"Glory," in both Hebrew and Greek, stands for the manifested presence of a person, in this case that of God or Christ. In both languages the term was used for the luminous cloud which appeared between the cherubim on the Ark of the Covenant (Lev. 16:2; Num. 16:42) and on rare occasions was said even to fill the entire Temple itself (I Kings 8:10-11). Peter has already suggested that Christians are to share in the "praise and glory and honor" of Christ at his appearing (1:7, 13), and no doubt he has that same eschatological event in mind in the present passage (vs. 13). At the same time, he appears to have also in mind that at the very time one is "reproached for the name of Christ," the blessing of "the spirit of glory and of God" is a present experience and "rests upon" the Christian in the very midst of his reproach (vs. 14).

By way of justifying the Christian's attitude in the face of the fiery ordeal, the reproach, and the suffering "for the name of Christ," Peter now returns to the thought of the coming Judgment. From the time of Amos forward, the prophets and other biblical writers had spoken of "the day of the LORD" or the Day of Judgment (Amos 5:18-20; Ezek. 30:1-3) as a future prospect. But Christians are conscious of the fact that even now they are living in the "last times," as we have already seen; "the end of all things is at hand" (vs. 7 above) and "the time has come for judgment to begin" (vs. 17). Also from the time of Amos forward the thought had been prominently expressed that God's people would be the first to experience his judgment (Amos 3:2). Peter voices his agreement with this thought when he says, "The time has come for judgment to begin with the household of God."

God's people, however, are not to expect anything other than impartiality on the part of God. If God's people are to be vindicated, it will be because they are prepared to "suffer according to God's will" and "do right and entrust their souls to a faithful Creator" (vs. 19). God's absolute demand that men "do right" regardless of consequences is justified, because God is the "faithful Creator" who fulfills his promises to his people, and therefore they may without reserve "entrust their souls" to him.

The warning to those "who do not obey the gospel of God" (vs. 17) may be taken as the equivalent of the previous warning to those who "disobey the word" (2:8; 3:1, 20). The word in all of these cases is the word as preached, the equivalent of the "gospel." This "word" or "gospel" contains an account not only of God's redemptive love but also of his wrath against the disobedient who do not accept that love. It is notable that here, as in Hebrews 3 and 4, "disobedience" is the cardinal sin because of which men are lost. Accordingly, in the quotation from Proverbs 11:31 (vs. 18) "the righteous man" who is "saved" is the one who accepts the gospel in faith, while "the impious and sinner" will be the one who rejects it and refuses to live out its implications for human living.

Consequent Duties of Christians (5:1-11)

In this final section of the letter, so much of which has been devoted to exhortation of one sort or another, Peter addresses various groups in the Christian community, particularly those whom he calls "elders" (vs. 1) and the "younger" people (vs. 5). At least the first of these groups represents persons holding some official status in the local communities, as Peter's description of himself as "a fellow elder" and his charge to them—"Tend the flock of God that is your charge" (vs. 2)—serve to indicate. In Judaism the "elder" was a leader in the synagogue as well as in some cases a member of the Sanhedrin (see Mark 8:31; Acts 4:5, 8; 6:12; 23:14). In the Greek world "elders" had both civic and religious duties, and a group of them might constitute the ruling body of the city. The Christian Church took over this office with its rich background, and in many communities it doubtless represented the sole leadership in the local Christian community (see Acts 14:23; 20:17).

That Peter should speak of himself here merely as "a fellow elder" rather than as an Apostle should not be considered strange. It would certainly have been unseemly for Peter to lack the very humility which he was about to enjoin upon his readers (vss. 5-6). Moreover, his apostolic authority is sufficiently cared for in the description of himself further as "a witness of the sufferings of Christ as well as a partaker in the glory that is to be revealed." Probably none of his readers could make a claim such as this (see 1:8). In any case, it was Peter's personal relation to Jesus Christ which made him an ambassador with full power of dispensing the gospel, or, as he prefers, "a witness" to the great facts of that gospel. It is to be noted that in this passage the twofold theme of "sufferings" and "glory" is carried through along the same lines as elsewhere in the letter (1:11; 2:21; 3:14-15, 18-22; 4:1, 13). The "elders" also are to share in these "sufferings of Christ" as they "tend the flock of God" in the expectation that they "will obtain the unfading crown of glory" along with him (vs. 4).

Their work is to be carried on under the supervision of "the chief Shepherd," a term nowhere else found in the New Testament, though the idea for which it stands is of course prominent in a number of passages (Mark 14:27; John 10:11; Heb. 13:20). The elders of the Church, therefore, are to think of themselves as shepherds serving under this "chief Shepherd," and the congregation allotted to their care is called "the flock of God" (vs. 2). The main characteristics of their service as undershepherds are to be willingness, eagerness, and lack of the domineering spirit which is so characteristic of those occupying a secular office. In general, the instruction given to these pastors is similar to that which Jesus gave to his own disciples, to whom he said that those who would be "first" should be "last," and that the leader should be as the "servant of all" (Mark 9:35).

The "younger," though the word is masculine in the Greek, may refer to younger people generally and is so understood by most students. A few commentators have thought that the word referred to officebearers, possibly the equivalent of "deacons" (see Acts 5:6). It is more likely, however, that the "younger" are here addressed as over against their "elders" in age, inasmuch as no suggestion is made regarding any function which they are to perform. Like all other members of the Christian community they are simply enjoined to "be subject," that is, to recognize the fact that in any community, including the Christian fellowship, law and order must be maintained. This same principle relates to all members of the community, as we have already seen (2:13—3:7).

Peter now speaks to the laity generally (vss. 5b-11), saying three things in particular. First, he says, "Clothe yourselves, all of you, with humility toward one another" (vs. 5). Already (2:13-17) such humility has been set in the context of God's over-all sovereignty with reference to "every human institution" (2:13; see Prov. 3:34). To observe such "humility toward one another" is actually to place oneself "under the mighty hand of God" (vs. 6). And Peter proceeds to suggest, very much after the manner of Jesus himself (Mark 10:35-45), that those who thus submit to the sovereignty of God are to expect that "in due time" he will "exalt" them.

Second, after the manner of Matthew 6:25-34, Peter suggests: "Cast all your anxieties on him, for he cares about you" (vs. 7). In view of the providential care of his Creator, the Christian is to live his life without undue anxiety.

Third, the Christian is to "be sober, be watchful" (vs. 8). This is like the teaching in I Thessalonians 5:6—a letter which Silvanus had a share in writing, as he did in the case of the present letter (vs. 12; see I Thess. 1:1). Such teaching, however, is found in numerous other passages in the New Testament and can be traced back to our Lord himself (Matt. 26:41; Mark 13:32-37).

The need of such sobriety and watchfulness is associated with the fact that "your adversary the devil prowls around like a roaring lion, seeking someone to devour." It seems clear that Peter here equates the work of "the devil" with the "experience of suffering" of which he has been speaking throughout the letter (vs. 9; see 4:12-14). This suffering is occasioned of course by men, and it would seem therefore that Peter uses the term "the devil" in a metaphorical sense to refer to the general and corporate evil of humanity with which the Christian "brotherhood throughout the world" has to deal.

The Christian is to remember that such suffering is for only "a little while" (vs. 10; see Heb. 10:37), that is, throughout the period remaining until "the God of all grace, who has called you to his eternal glory in Christ, will himself restore, establish, and strengthen you." The teaching here is very similar to that in I Thessalonians 5:1-11 and II Thessalonians 2:1-12, the two letters in which Silvanus also had a part. The hortatory and didactic portion of the epistle now ends with a suitable doxology in verse 11.

CLOSING GREETINGS
I Peter 5:12-14

As we have already noted, this letter is almost exclusively exhortation (vs. 12; see also Heb. 13:22). "Silvanus," the name of Peter's amanuensis or stenographer, is a Latin form and probably is to be equated with the Greek "Silas." This Silas was originally a man of prominence in the Jerusalem church (Acts 15:22, 27, 32). He became a companion of Paul on his missionary journeys (Acts 15:40; 16:19, 25, 29; 17:4; 18:5), and Paul associated him with himself in his preaching (II Cor. 1:19) and writing (I Thess. 1:1; II Thess. 1:1). That Peter should use the Latin form of his name may have some connection with the fact that "Babylon" is possibly a pseudonym employed by Peter for "Rome" (vs. 13; see Rev. 14:8). The "Mark" referred to is the John Mark of Acts 12:12, 25; 13:5, 13; 15:37. His mother Mary maintained a house in Jerusalem which was a center for the early Jerusalem Christian community (Acts 12:12). He was a relative of Barnabas and accompanied Paul on some of his missionary labors (Col. 4:10; II Tim. 4:11; Philemon 24). Later tradition associates him also with the work of Peter, and identifies him as the latter's interpreter.

The "kiss of love" or "holy kiss" (vs. 14) is also suggested by Paul as appropriate among Christians (Rom. 16:16; I Cor. 16:20; II Cor. 13:12; I Thess. 5:26). It was apparently a form of salutation or greeting taken over by the Church from contemporary Judaism (Luke 7:45; 22:48). Peter's closing greeting ("Peace to all of you that are in Christ") is a variation of the usual contemporary Semitic formula, "Peace be with you," or "Peace to you" (see 1:2).

THE SECOND LETTER OF

PETER

INTRODUCTION

Composition and Style of the Letter

As a literary form Second Peter approaches Hebrews and Ephesians more nearly than any other of the writings of the New Testament. All are essentially "essays" or "sermons." If it were not for the fact that in 1:1-2 and 3:1-2 the suggestion is made by the author that he is in fact writing a letter which is addressed to the Church, we should never have suspected that this little piece of literature was other than either essay or homily. Probably, therefore, we should think of it as originally composed by its author to serve as an address to be delivered to a particular congregation. Thereafter, either he or another may have superimposed upon it the letter form which it now assumes.

The style of this letter or essay is quite unlike that of its sister epistle, First Peter. First Peter was written by one who knew good vernacular Greek and who could probably speak and think in the Greek language, the lingua franca of the day. Second Peter is written in the artificial, stilted manner of one who is endeavoring to copy the literary or semi-literary fashion of his contemporaries. The vocabulary of Second Peter is as remarkable as its style, consisting to some extent of high-sounding words, 57 of which are not found elsewhere in the New Testament. On the whole, the author produces the impression of one who was not well acquainted with the Greek language or who may have learned it rather late in life from reading rather than as a medium for speaking.

Closely related to the matter of style, and by no means to be divorced from it, is the fact that Second Peter employed portions of other New Testament writings, altering them considerably to conform to his artificial literary style. There can be no doubt, for example, that he has used First Peter and Jude in this way, and possibly also the Gospel of Luke or the tradition lying behind it (see comment on 1:18), as well as Romans and Hebrews (see comment on 2:19-22).

Again related to matters of style and composition is the fact that Second Peter makes no use of the Greek Old Testament, a phenomenon remarkable in itself among New Testament writings. The one quotation is at 2:22 (see Prov. 26:11), and this quotation approximates more nearly to the Hebrew than to the Greek translation. In addition, there are five citations of Old Testament incidents (see 2:4, 5, 6, 7, 15-16), but none of these contains an actual quotation from either the Hebrew or the Greek, and all five occur in the passage taken over almost bodily from Jude.

Circumstances, Message, and Date of the Letter

Circumstances

Though we have no certain way of knowing who the hearers were for whom this essay or sermon was prepared, or who the readers were to whom it was addressed, the circumstances in which they find themselves are clear. They are being brought under the influence of "false teachers" (2:1), who are delivering themselves of "destructive heresies" and whose lives are characterized by "licentiousness" (2:2, 13-16).

The sort of teaching which the letter warns against follows roughly the pattern of what is called for want of a better name "Gnosticism." The term stands for a loosely organized type of religious belief which in the early centuries drew to itself both oriental and occidental elements. It was constantly in a state of flux and did not develop into rigid forms until the third and fourth centuries. But it represents a type of philosophical and religious thinking which has perennially proved attractive to a certain type of mind. The word itself derives from the Greek word for "knowledge," and it is no doubt significant that Second Peter makes much of a Christian type of "knowledge" which may be thought to stand over against that paraded by the "false teachers" (see 1:2, 3, 5, 6, 8; 2:20; 3:18).

In the above-mentioned respects, the "false teachers" of Second Peter were generally like those against whom Jude wrote. Their "licentiousness" and arrogance were due to the fact that they pretended to possess an esoteric knowledge in spiritual matters which placed them above the necessity of living true moral lives. It was characteristic of Gnosticism of every sort to separate religion and morals, as having no necessary connection the one with the other. This was because the Gnostics believed that only soul or spirit was made up of fine elements which could be saved, while matter and body were so crudely formed as to be unworthy and incapable of salvation. In consequence some boasted of the ability to indulge in "licentious passions of the flesh" without endangering the spirit's salvation (2:18; see Jude 8).

Unlike the false teachers of Jude's time, however, those discussed in Second Peter scoff particularly at the thought of the "coming" of Jesus Christ and of "the day of judgment" which will succeed it (3:3-7).

Message

The message of Second Peter is based upon "the prophetic word" (1:19) and "the predictions of the holy prophets" (3:2), as these find support in the apostolic witness (1:12-18; 3:2). The content of this message is "the knowledge of God and of Jesus our Lord" (1:2), which enables Christians to escape from "the corruption that is in the world because of passion" and to become "partakers of the divine nature" (1:4), and which flowers in a type of genuine ethical living quite other than the licentiousness which characterized the current Gnosticism (1:5-11).

This unique Christian "knowledge of God" gives the author a standard by which he may condemn the "false teachers" (2:1-22). On the basis of such "knowledge of God" as the Christian possesses (see comment on 3:1-13) he is also able to reply to their scoffing at the idea of the coming of our Lord and the Judgment. He rounds out his essay-letter with an exhortation to right ethical living (3:14-18).

Date

The date of writing of Second Peter is by no means easy to determine. As is shown in the comment, the author seems to have been acquainted with the teaching of Romans and Hebrews (2:19-22) and with the collection of Paul's letters generally (3:15-16), with the Gospel of Luke (1:16-18) and possibly with that of Matthew (1:17), and with Jude (2:1-18; 3:2-3). Accordingly, it is obvious that the letter's date is later than those assigned to the other writings.

Further, the author clearly places himself and his readers in a period succeeding the passing away of at least the first generation of Christians (3:4). Then, too, there is little if any evidence of Second Peter's having been used by Christian writers before the middle or third quarter of the second century. For these reasons most interpreters of the letter date it sometime after the beginning or even in the middle of the second century.

The arguments advanced for this late date are not entirely conclusive. Since the discovery of the Qumran Scrolls there is a rather general tendency to assign an earlier date than previously to some of the key writings of the New Testament. This tendency has already affected the problem of dating some of the writings mentioned above and may eventually affect all of them. In consequence, it is less certain than appeared to be the case some years ago, that we need assign to this letter a date after A.D. 70.

Authorship of the Letter

It is almost universally held among interpreters of Second Peter that its author was not the Apostle Peter. Most would probably agree that the letter is an example of the pseudonymous literature which arose about his name and was given his authority from the middle of the second century onward. As a comparison of First Peter with Second Peter shows abundantly, the Greek style, nature of composition of the two letters, and their respective messages differ radically.

If it be agreed that Silvanus did the major work in composing First Peter as its coauthor (see Introduction to First Peter), then it may be allowed that there are certain factors (though these are admittedly not entirely conclusive) favoring the Petrine authorship of Second Peter. For example, in 1:1 the author writes as a Jewish Christian might well write to Gentile Christians (note "ours" and "those"). This observation accords with the fact that in the only quotation made from the Old Testament in the letter (2:22), the author appears to be translating directly from the Hebrew of Proverbs 26:11, rather than employing the common Greek translation. This may suggest that he was better acquainted with the Old Testament in Hebrew than in Greek. Further, his use of Jude and his reference to the Pauline letters might be argued as in favor of the author's being the Apostle Peter rather than another. It is unlikely that a Galilean fisherman would know much about the contemporary Gnostic teaching, and it should not surprise us that in answering such teaching he should lean upon others as the author apparently does. Furthermore, the author's humility, as shown in his attitude toward the Pauline letters, is what one might expect from the genuine Peter (3:15-16; see Gal. 2:11-14). Again, expressions like "the knowledge of God and of Jesus our Lord" (1:2), "the way of righteousness," and "the holy commandment" (2:21) are what one might well expect from a Jewish Christian such as the Apostle Peter. Finally, it is to be observed that we lack criteria (other than such passages from Jesus' teaching as Luke 12:39-40 and from Paul's at I Thessalonians 5:2-11) for knowing what the earliest disciples may have thought on the subject of the Second Coming. And inasmuch as at this point Second Peter agrees with such teachings (see 3:8-10), this would seem to argue in favor of the apostolic authorship of the letter. In view of these considerations, the possibility of the Petrine authorship of Second Peter cannot be denied, any more than can the possibility of its early date. For these reasons it is best to leave the matter of authorship and date open, in the hope that future discoveries may throw more light upon the problem.

OUTLINE

Salutation. II Peter 1:1-2

The Knowledge of God. II Peter 1:3—3:13
    The Knowledge of God in Jesus Christ (1:3-11)
    Sources of the Knowledge of God (1:12-21)
    Denial of the Knowledge of God (2:1—3:13)

Exhortation to Righteous Living. II Peter 3:14-18

COMMENTARY

SALUTATION

II Peter 1:1-2

Like First Peter, Second Peter opens with a salutation closely resembling Paul's modification of the usual opening of the Greek letter of that day. The naming of Peter as author of the letter differs in two respects from that employed in I Peter 1:1—first, in joining Peter's original Aramaic name of "Simon" with his Greek name (see Matt. 16:17; John 1:42); and second, in describing Peter as "a servant" as well as an "apostle of Jesus Christ." In this respect also Second Peter is somewhat patterned after Paul's formula (see Rom. 1:1).

Unlike First Peter (see 1:1), Second Peter is not addressed to any particular group of churches, but instead is written to "those who have obtained a faith of equal standing with ours in the righteousness of our God and Savior Jesus Christ" (vs. 1). This unusual description of the readers of the letter, together with its general format and the fact that it contains no closing greetings, suggests that in origin it was an essay or sermon, later converted into a letter by the addition of the opening salutation. However, as we shall see, the stamp of Peter's experiences and character is so impressed upon the composition as a whole as to point to its essential unity and to the fact that it must have been the original author—whoever he may have been, Peter or another—who superimposed upon the essay the letter form in the name of Peter (see 1:14, 17-18; 3:1-2).

"Faith" plays a relatively small part in the teaching of Second Peter, the word being found only in verses 1 and 5 of this first chapter, whereas in First Peter it is found in 1:5, 7, 9, 21, and 5:9. Nowhere else in the New Testament is "faith" said to be "in the righteousness of our God and Savior Jesus Christ," the nearest equivalent to this expression being found in Galatians 5:5 (see also Rom. 1:17). The idea however, is a thoroughly biblical one, inasmuch as "righteousness' in the Scriptures represents a far more concrete conception than with us. We might, therefore, translate the Greek here rather as "faith . . . in the righteous activity" of God, such activity being the equivalent of the "sal-

vation" or "deliverance" which he works out for man on the plane
of history through a series of redemptive acts (see Isa. 51:5, 6,
8).

The first part of the benediction in verse 2 ("May grace and
peace be multiplied to you") is identical with that found in I Peter
1:2 (see comment). In what follows in this verse ("in the knowledge of God and of Jesus our Lord") we are introduced to two
points of striking significance for the letter as a whole—first, its
emphasis upon "knowledge," and second, its high view of the
person of Jesus Christ. This is seen here in the close connection of
"God" and "Jesus our Lord," a phenomenon which is duplicated
many times elsewhere in the New Testament (see I Cor. 8:6). The
expression "our God and Savior Jesus Christ" in verse 1, however, goes beyond the one in verse 2. It is comparable in form to
the expression "our Lord and Savior Jesus Christ" in 1:11; 2:20;
and 3:18 (see also 3:2). There can be no doubt that in these latter references "Lord" and "Savior" both apply to "Jesus Christ,"
and it is natural, therefore, to take the expression "God and Savior"
as also referring to "Jesus Christ," as is done in the Revised
Standard Version. The only other New Testament passage in
which Jesus Christ is called at once God and Savior is Titus
2:13.

THE KNOWLEDGE OF GOD
II Peter 1:3—3:13

The Knowledge of God in Jesus Christ (1:3-11)
Knowledge Leads to Partaking of the Divine Nature (1:3-4)

One of the most striking characteristics of Second Peter (and
one incidentally which distinguishes it markedly from First Peter)
is the emphasis upon "knowledge." Two Greek words, both from
the same stem, are translated in this way in the Revised Standard
Version. The more simple of the two, the word which gives us
"Gnosticism," is found in 1:5, 6 and 3:18; its verb form (to
"understand") appears in 1:20 and 3:3. The related word, also
translated "knowledge," is found in 1:2, 3, 8, and 2:20, and its
verbal form appears twice in 2:21, where it is translated "known"
and "knowing." None of these forms with the exception of the
very first is found in First Peter (see I Peter 3:7, "considerately"),

and this one instance has no theological significance. In Second Peter the "knowledge" in question concerns, in the first instance, an intimate acquaintance and fellowship with God, or, alternatively, with Jesus Christ as Lord. In the New Testament the nearest approach to Second Peter's meaning is to be found in numerous passages in Paul (see Rom. 1:28; 10:2; Eph. 1:17; 4:13).

In verses 3-4 Peter's thesis is that this intimate "knowledge" of God is the means whereby men are led to share his "glory and excellence," thus receiving the fulfillment of "his precious and very great promises" and at last becoming "partakers of the divine nature." The creative cause, says our author, which lies behind this redemptive process is God's "divine power." The expressions "divine power" and "divine nature," which represent at once the beginning and end of this redemptive activity of God, find no parallel in the New Testament, but the ideas involved are biblical. It needs no proof that throughout the Scriptures the power of God lies behind the redemptive process. And it is clear that for Second Peter, to be "partakers of the divine nature" is simply to say that God has "called us to his own glory and excellence"—a wholly biblical idea (see Rom. 2:10; 5:2; 8:21; I Cor. 2:7; II Cor. 3:18).

In the phrase "his own glory and excellence" we probably have a form of expression where two words are used to express a single idea. In Isaiah 42:8 and 12 the Greek translation of the Hebrew (rendered in the Revised Standard Version "glory" and "praise") employs the same two Greek words as are found here. "Excellence," therefore, should be taken to mean the same as "glory," and both together represent the fact that, by the "divine power," man is to be raised to the stature of the manifested nature of God in all of his moral excellence (see Eph. 4:13). The statement that God gives his people "all things that pertain to life and godliness" sounds very much like the teaching of Jesus, as for example, in Matthew 6:33 and 7:11. God's salvation of man issues in "escape from . . . corruption" and the effects of man's "passion" (see also 2:10, 18; 3:3).

Confirmation of Election by Ethical Living (1:5-11)

The title of this section might equally have been "confirmation of *faith* by ethical living," inasmuch as it opens with the suggestion that the readers should "make every effort to supplement . . . [their] faith with virtue" (vs. 5). The thesis which is developed here is that one's theology or religion should be followed up

by ethical living appropriate to it. And in this respect the teaching is like that of Paul in Romans and Ephesians. For in these
two letters the earlier chapters (Rom. 1-11; Eph. 1-3) are devoted to theology, and as the "therefore" (Rom. 12:1 and Eph.
4:1) indicates, the ethical exhortations which follow are based
upon the sound theology which precedes. Second Peter's "for this
very reason" in the present section has the same effect as Paul's
"therefore."

The general teaching of the passage is to the effect that the
Christian's "faith" should blossom in right ethical living, in order
that his "knowledge of our Lord Jesus Christ" (vs. 8) might not
prove "ineffective or unfruitful," but that rather he should show
himself as one "cleansed from his old sins" (vs. 9) and so "con-
firm . . . [his] call and election" (vs. 10). The ultimate end or goal
of this confirmation of the Christian's "faith" and "election," says
Second Peter, is that he may find "entrance into the eternal kingdom of our Lord and Savior Jesus Christ" (vs. 11).

Here for the first time we have a reference to the eschatological perspective which is fundamental to the thought of our author.
As we shall see, this perspective dominates his thought from verse
16 onward to the end of the letter, and more particularly in chapters 2 and 3. In this respect his teaching approximates closely that
of First Peter (see I Peter 1:3, 7, 11, 13; 3:21-22; 4:6, 7-11, 13-
14; 5:10). The phrase "eternal kingdom" appears nowhere else
in the New Testament, the nearest approach to it being in Luke
16:9 ("eternal habitations") and in II Corinthians 5:1 ("a house
not made with hands, eternal in the heavens"). The author may
have in mind, of course, Jesus' teaching in Mark 10:15 and the
Johannine concept of "eternal life" (John 3:15-16), and there is
even some remote relation to Paul's teaching in I Corinthians
15:24, 28.

Somewhat similar lists of the ethical implications of "faith"
(vss. 5-7) are to be found in Romans 5:1-5; Galatians 5:22-23;
Ephesians 5:9; I Timothy 6:11. Paul terms all of these "the fruit
of the Spirit" (Gal. 5:22), and Second Peter has already expressed
the similar idea that they proceed from God's "divine power" (vs.
3). Nonetheless, for both Paul and Second Peter, man is to put
forth "every effort" to see that the ethical life matches his religious
faith (vs. 5; see Rom. 6:11-23). "Virtue" (vs. 5) refers to the
"excellence" of man's character and activity which give expression
to his "faith." "Self-control" was a virtue much admired by the

Stoics and other Greeks, but it had already been baptized into
Christian usage by the Church (see Acts 24:25; I Cor. 9:25; and
Gal. 5:23). In Christian thought it is the natural outcome of complete surrender to the lordship of God over one's life (Matt. 6:33;
Rom. 6:17-18, 22). Ethical living, says Second Peter, is a clear
indication of the Christian's not forgetting that he has been
"cleansed from his old sins" (vs. 9). This is a favorite teaching of
the Apostle Paul also (Rom. 6:1-11; 8:1-11; Gal. 5:13-24; see
also I Peter 4:1-6). The idea that the ordinary Christian receives
a "call and election" from God (vs. 10) was also a common doctrine of the Church by the time Second Peter was written (for
"call" see Matt. 22:14; Mark 2:17; Rom. 8:30; I Cor. 1:26; 7:20;
Gal. 1:6; and for "election," Matt. 22:14; Luke 18:7; Rom. 8:33;
Col. 3:12; I Thess. 1:4).

Sources of the Knowledge of God (1:12-21)

The Apostolic Witness (1:12-18)

The remainder of chapter 1 is devoted to a discussion of the
sources of the knowledge of God about which the author has been
writing in verses 3-11. These sources are: first, the Apostles (note
"we" in vss. 16-19), and second, the prophets (vs. 19). In at-
tributing the knowledge of God which was the possession of the
early Christian Church to the Apostles and to the prophets before
them, Second Peter is in line with the teaching of First Peter (see
I Peter 1:10-12 and 5:1).

The author first describes the apostolic witness which lies behind the Church's knowledge of God, and in so doing he identifies
himself with the Apostle Peter (vs. 14; see John 21:18-19). He
declares that "the putting off of . . . [his] body" (which the "Lord
Jesus Christ showed" him) would occur "soon." In other words,
he writes as Peter would have written in his old age and when
conscious of the fact that the end was near. He speaks of his witness as merely a "reminder" (vs. 13; see also vs. 12 and 3:1). It
is clear that he does not think of himself as giving his readers
the great gospel facts for the first time, for they already "know
them and are established in the truth" with regard to them (vs.
12; see 3:1-2). His "reminder"—or, as it were, his memorandum
—is made with a view to their being able after his "departure . . .
at any time to recall these things" (vs. 15).

To demonstrate the validity of his witness as a source of the knowledge of God, the author selects out of numerous possible experiences that one when Peter with his two associates was "with him [that is, Jesus] on the holy mountain" of transfiguration (vs. 18). Here Peter and his associates had been "eyewitnesses of his majesty" (vs. 16), a "majesty" the like of which Jesus in his incarnate life had not hitherto assumed. And he would not again assume such "majesty" until the second "coming" (vs. 16), when the event would be accompanied with unique "power."

This witness which the author proclaims is no doubt to be identified with the "truth," which he says in verse 12 his readers have already come to possess. Such identification of the apostolic witness or gospel with "the truth" is a common phenomenon in the New Testament (see John 5:33; 8:32; Gal. 2:5; Eph. 1:13). In II Timothy 4:4 and Titus 1:14, this "truth" of the gospel is contrasted, as in verse 16, with "cleverly devised myths." Both Jews and Gentiles, as the other two references suggest, knew and propagated such myths devised to express or undergird religious teachings. The author's clear intention is to deny that the Christian faith must look for support to such a worthless mythology. Rather, like the prophetic faith taught in all of Scripture, it is founded upon eyewitness testimony to the redemptive activity of God on the plane of history.

The Prophetic Word (1:19-21)

The second source of information (actually the first chronologically) of the "knowledge" of God, of which the author has been speaking, is "the prophetic word" (vs. 19). In the context of the author's thought and the situation in which he is writing, this "prophetic word" is of an eschatological nature and has as its content the "coming" of Jesus Christ (see vs. 16). The Transfiguration has "made more sure," through its revelation of the "glory" of Jesus Christ, the fact of his coming; it is a sort of foretaste of the glory of Christ which will be his at his coming again.

The author warns his readers that they "will do well to pay attention" to this prophecy regarding Jesus' coming again, inasmuch as "no prophecy ever came by the impulse of man" (vs. 21). Rather, the prophets were "men moved by the Holy Spirit" and they, therefore, "spoke from God." It is not too much to say that to his mind the prophets and Apostles were on a par as instruments of revelation. A comparison of verses 18 and 21 with each other makes this clear; the Apostles had a "voice borne from heaven" to them, and similarly the prophets were recipients of the "Holy Spirit" and in consequence "spoke from God."

Second Peter's suggestion further that "no prophecy of scripture is a matter of one's own interpretation" (vs. 20) is quite clearly intended as a basic principle to be used in replying to the "scoffers" (see 3:3) with whom he is about to deal. Verses 20 and 21 taken together are intended to say that only the "Holy Spirit," through whom the prophetic word comes, is capable of interpreting that word. In consequence, his readers are forewarned that it is their duty to discover *through whom* Scripture is being properly interpreted in their generation.

In verse 19 "the day" which is about to dawn is the day of consummation, of judgment, of the coming of Jesus Christ (see Amos 5:18; Mark 13:32; I Thess. 5:2). The Greek word here translated "the morning star" occurs nowhere else in the New Testament; "the morning star" in Revelation 2:28 and "the bright morning star" in Revelation 22:16 represent other Greek expressions. However, the latter gives us the key to the author's meaning, as it is Jesus who is there speaking as he says, "I am the root and the offspring of David, the bright morning star" (see Isa. 11:1, 10). In any case, when the author combines two expressions such as "the day dawns" and "the morning star rises in your hearts," he is rather obviously referring at one and the same time to a general future fact (the "coming of our Lord Jesus Christ," vs. 16) and to a personal experience (the same Jesus' "coming" in one's own life). This combination need not seem strange to us, in view of the fact that the author had seen in his own experience of the Transfiguration an anticipation of the Final Coming.

Denial of the Knowledge of God (2:1—3:13)

Existence of False Prophets and False Teachers (2:1-22)

It is rather generally agreed that in his description of the "false teachers" (vs. 1), their "heresies" and their "licentiousness" (vs. 2), the author is relying on and employing the little Letter of Jude (particularly vss. 4-13, 18). We shall not attempt here a detailed comparison of the two letters. But the student should notice that in general the "false teachers" are described as "denying the

Master who bought them" (vs. 1; see Jude 4), and as indulging in unethical conduct which both authors describe as a crude "licentiousness" (vs. 2; see Jude 4). In both letters these undesirable teachers who have made entry into the Christian Church are characterized as arrogant "scoffers" (3:3; see Jude 18), and in both their "condemnation" or "destruction" is threatened (vss. 3, 17; 3:7; see Jude 13, 22-23). It should be noted, too, that many of the illustrations of rebellion against God cited by the two authors are the same, for example, the fallen angels (vs. 4; Jude 6), Sodom and Gomorrah (vs. 6; Jude 7), and Balaam (vs. 15; Jude 11). Much of the phraseology employed by the authors to describe the "false teachers" is similar, if not identical; for example, they "revile the glorious ones" (vs. 10; Jude 8) and act like "irrational animals" (vs. 12; see Jude 10); they are described as "blemishes" in their "carousing" (vs. 13; Jude 12) and are "waterless springs and mists driven by a storm" (vs. 17; Jude 12), for whom "the nether gloom of darkness has been reserved" (vs. 17; Jude 13). This is by no means an exhaustive list of the similarities between the two letters, but it will perhaps serve to suggest the likelihood that Second Peter employs Jude's description of these "false teachers," since that description suits his purpose.

In 2:1-3 the author is concerned to suggest that his readers should remember how at all times in the history of the people of God the true and the false are found together, and that a choice must be made by this people. Just as in the past "false prophets" were found along with those who had the prophetic word in their mouths, so now there are "false teachers" to be distinguished from the true (see Matt. 7:15-23). From the description of these false teachers, it seems clear that they were of the type loosely described as "Gnostic." Such teachers arose within both Judaism and Christianity and drew their teachings from a multitude of sources. Like the modern "theosophists," they were eclectics—that is, they selected from here and there teachings congenial to their own thinking. They were generally arrogant, holding that they alone were in possession of the "way of truth" (vs. 2), and their arrogance was usually matched with "licentiousness" or immoral living.

In verses 4-10 the author enlarges on the idea expressed in verse 3, to the effect that the "false teachers" will discover that "their condemnation has not been idle, and their destruction has not been asleep." He selects three outstanding examples from the patriarchal times in proof of his thesis—namely, "the angels when they sinned" (vs. 4; see Gen. 6:1-4); "the ancient world" at the time of the flood (vs. 5; Gen. 6:5-7); and finally, the "turning the cities of Sodom and Gomorrah to ashes" (vs. 6; Gen. 19:24-25). Second Peter's argument from these three examples is that God "knows how . . . to keep the unrighteous under punishment until the day of judgment" (vs. 9). At the same time, he also cites the cases of Noah (vs. 5; Gen. 6:8-22; 8:20-22) and Lot (vss. 7-8; Gen. 19:15-23), to indicate that the Lord "knows how to rescue the godly from trial" (vs. 9).

The reference in verse 4 to the fallen "angels" (see Jude 6) arises from the fact that the Greek translation of Genesis 6:1-4, instead of "sons of God," reads "angels of God." This teaching about the fallen angels was greatly elaborated in the apocryphal book of First Enoch, with which either Jude or Second Peter or both seem to have been familiar. This book teaches that for their sin these angels were "cast . . . into hell and committed . . . to pits of nether gloom to be kept until the judgment" (vs. 4; see I Enoch 10:4-13). Jude does not refer to the case of Noah, and probably Second Peter derived the reference to him, and the "seven other persons" with him, from I Peter 3:20. Similarly, although the example of "Sodom and Gomorrah" is found in both Second Peter and Jude (vs. 6; Jude 7), that of the "righteous Lot" is found nowhere else in the New Testament except in Luke 17:28-32, where Noah also is cited as an example (vss. 26-27).

The two sins which are particularly abhorrent to the author and which he sees illustrated in the examples he has cited, he now specifies as indulgence in "the lust of defiling passion" and as the tendency to "despise authority" (vs. 10). He has already spoken of these two sins, employing a slightly different terminology, in verses 1-3, and he will further develop his picture of the contemporary "false teachers" along these two lines.

Verses 10b-18 follow very closely the text of Jude 8-13. Like Jude (see Jude 8-10), Second Peter says that the false teachers, "bold and wilful," do not hesitate to "revile the glorious ones" (vs. 10b). These false teachers are then compared with "angels" who do not indulge in such "reviling" (vs. 11), and with "irrational animals" in their "reviling in matters of which they are ignorant" (vs. 12). It is not clear to what event the author has reference here. Jude has a more specific reference to "the archangel Michael" at this point, and he says that, while "contending

with the devil . . . about the body of Moses," Michael refrained
from reviling the latter. Instead, the archangel merely said, "The
Lord rebuke you" (Jude 9; see Zech. 3:2). No such incident is
recorded anywhere in Scripture, and it has been assumed by some
that Jude (and, following him less precisely, Second Peter) is
citing here an incident recorded in the lost apocryphal book, The
Assumption of Moses. However this may be, in both letters it is
the arrogance of the false teachers upon which stress is laid. They
"will be destroyed . . . suffering wrong for their wrongdoing"
(vss. 12-13).

The second sin of the false teachers is variously described by
both Second Peter and Jude as "reveling," "carousing," "adultery,"
and "greed" (vss. 13-18; Jude 11-13). Jude actually suggests that
this reveling was carried on at the "love feasts" of the Christians
(Jude 12). And some of our best manuscripts read "their love
feasts" instead of "their dissipation" (vs. 13; see margin). The
difference in the Greek words involved amounts only to a change
of two letters! Paul also is witness to the fact of such scandalous
reveling on the occasion of the Lord's Supper (see I Cor. 11:21).
It seems unbelievable that any Christians, however heretical,
should have converted the most sacred of Christian rituals into a
debauchery. And yet we must recall that many of these Christians, particularly those who had come out of a pagan environ-
ment, were not far removed from their former manner of living.

The example of "Balaam," to whom reference is made by both
Second Peter and Jude (vss. 15-16; Jude 11; Num. 22-24), and
who in both letters is taken as an example of one who "loved gain
from wrongdoing," is striking. This is particularly so because in
Revelation 2:14 it is said that in the church at Pergamum in the
Roman province of Asia a like "teaching of Balaam" was found.
Second Peter follows the account in Numbers in implying that the
"dumb ass" (vs. 16) had more prophetic insight than the prophet
whom he bore! Like Jude, the author suggests that such teachers
are merely "waterless springs," "mists driven by a storm," and
that for them the same "nether gloom of darkness has been reserved" as for the fallen angels (vss. 17-18; see vs. 4 and Jude
12-13). We are reminded of Paul's description of immaturity as
characterized by being "tossed to and fro and carried about with
every wind of doctrine" (Eph. 4:14), and of the sins of the Gentiles who "have given themselves up to licentiousness, greedy to
practice every kind of uncleanness" (see Eph. 4:17-24).

The general teaching of verses 19-22 is that these false teachers are men who cannot distinguish liberty from license. They have tasted somewhat of the "freedom" of the Christian faith but they have used that freedom to become "slaves of corruption" (vs. 19). This is the type of thinking and acting which in the terminology of Christian ethics is called "antinomianism," that is, the teaching that freedom from the Law means that one is now free to do as he pleases, rather than as God pleases. Paul had to write against this sort of teaching, and in Romans 6 he made Second Peter's point that "whatever overcomes a man, to that he is enslaved" (vs. 19; see Rom. 6:16-18). According to the Fourth Gospel, Jesus had said very much the same thing (see John 8:34). It is generally believed that the "Nicolaitans" held to such antinomian teaching within the Christian Church (see Rev. 2:6, 14-15).

Verses 20-22 set forth the thesis that those who attain the freedom of the Christian "through the knowledge of our Lord and Savior Jesus Christ" and then turn back to the "defilements of the world" are worse off than they were before; "the last state has become worse for them than the first" (vs. 20). This teaching also has a familiar ring about it. For the sentence just quoted is almost an exact quotation of Matthew 12:45, and essentially the same teaching is also found in Hebrews 6:1-8. In verse 21 the two phrases "the way of righteousness" and "the holy commandment delivered to them," which clearly refer to the Christian gospel and its implications for ethical living, appear to be peculiar to Second Peter in the New Testament, although somewhat similar terms with essentially the same meaning are found elsewhere (see Matt. 7:13-14; John 13:34; 15:12; compare Rom. 7:12). In verse 22 the first part of the proverb ("The dog turns back to his own vomit") is probably taken from Proverbs 26:11, but the combination of the "dog" and the "sow" sounds very much like Matthew 7:6.

But if there is nothing new in the present section, it is at least informative of the hazardous state of the Church when it is surrounded by the defilements of a pagan society. The author, like the Apostle Paul, saw clearly the dire need of warning his readers that the Christian ethic follows naturally from the Christian theology. "You shall be holy, for I am holy" expresses this relationship as it is assumed throughout the totality of the Old and New Testament Scriptures (Lev. 19:2; see I Peter 1:16). The teaching of this section may be conveniently summed up in the words of

I Peter 2:16: "Live as free men, yet without using your freedom as a pretext for evil."

Scoffers at the Final Coming and the Judgment (3:1-4)

In addition to "denying the Master who bought them" (2:1) and so "the knowledge of our Lord and Savior Jesus Christ" (2:20), the false teachers also are found to be "scoffers" at the thought of the final coming of Jesus Christ as the Judge and Savior of men (vss. 3-4). It is this hostile attitude toward the Church's eschatological teaching with which the author deals in the closing chapter of his letter. He opens his discussion of this problem with references to the two major sources upon which he has been relying— namely, to First Peter (vs. 1), and to Jude, which he follows closely in 3:2-3 (Jude 17-18). And as before (see 1:12-15), he remarks that his own task is merely to arouse "your sincere mind by way of reminder" (vs. 1) of both "the predictions of the holy prophets" and "the commandment of the Lord and Savior through . . . [their] apostles" (vs. 2).

It is important to notice the exact way in which the problem is phrased by the "scoffers" whom the author wishes to answer. They refer to "the promise of his coming" (vs. 4), and they set this promise in the context of the fact that they are second or third generation Christians. The letter was quite evidently written at a day when it could be said that "the fathers" had fallen "asleep"; that is to say, the first generation had all died. The way in which the problem is stated implies that there was a group in the contemporary Christian community who believed that Jesus had predicted his "coming" as to be fulfilled within the lifetime of "the fathers." This manner of stating the problem, therefore, raises a twofold question: first, whether Jesus made any prediction at all with reference to his "coming"; and second, if he did, whether it was intended to have a specific time reference pertaining to the generation of "the fathers." Second Peter accepts by implication the contention that Jesus had made a general promise of his coming. However, he appears equally to imply in his answer that Jesus had never made any stipulation as to the time of the promise's fulfillment.

Second Peter's Reply to the Scoffers (3:5-13)

The first answer of our author to the scoffers is of a logical nature. And it is based upon two assumptions which underlie the teaching of the prophetic Scriptures with regard to the relation of God to his universe—namely, first, the thought that God is Sovereign over his world, and second, that as the beginning of the world was with "water," its end will be with "fire."

The first of these assumptions (that God is Sovereign over his universe) may be said to be *the most fundamental postulate of the Scriptures with regard to God.* "God is Lord" is as surely the basic statement of the Old Testament as "Jesus is Lord" is that of the New Testament (see Deut. 6:4-5; I Cor. 12:3). Because God is Sovereign, therefore, he is is also at once Creator and Judge. This is Second Peter's meaning as he writes that the scoffers "deliberately ignore" the fact that "by the word of God heavens existed long ago, and an earth formed out of water and by means of water" (vs. 5)—that is, *God is Creator;* and similarly, the fact that "by the same word the heavens and earth that now exist have been stored up for fire, being kept until the day of judgment and destruction of ungodly men" (vs. 7)—that is, *God is Judge of all the creation which he has made.*

The second postulate, which is equally prophetic with the first, is to the effect that the earth was formed out of "water," that is, was in a liquid state at the beginning, but that this water was not sufficient finally to destroy creation. It is true that "the world that then existed was deluged with water and perished" (vs. 6), but this perishing was merely a passing phase and not the end of creation (for this reference to the Flood see Gen. 8:20-22). For out of the creation there were preserved "the heavens and earth that now exist," and these are subject to God's ultimate judgment by "fire."

This prophetic conception of "water" as the material employed by the "word of God" at creation, and of "fire" as the destructive agency by which the "heavens and earth" will eventually be judged, is carried through extensively in the apocalyptic literature. In the New Testament itself the Revelation to John provides many examples of the place of water over against fire. Thus, for example, "the river of the water of life" plays a leading part in the creation of the new heavens and the new earth (Rev. 22:1-2); while fire (Rev. 16:8; 17:16), or "the lake of fire" (Rev. 19:20; 20:10), or even the "sea of glass mingled with fire" before the throne of God (Rev. 15:2), stands for the destructive force resident in God's creation. No doubt, too, the contrast between the baptisms of John and of Jesus as being, on the one hand, with

"water," and on the other, with "fire," reflects this type of pro-
phetic-apocalyptic contrast between the two elements (see Matt.
3:11).

On the basis of these two prophetic postulates, then, Second
Peter argues that the sovereign God of the universe will, of
course, judge and destroy all of his creation (including "ungodly
men") that he finds to be unworthy of his salvation (vs. 7).

Second Peter's second argument against the "scoffers" and their
views with regard to the Final Coming and the Judgment represents his most original contribution to this subject. He derives it
from Psalm 90:4, though he does not quote the Psalm as it appears in either the Hebrew or the Greek. In both those languages
the psalmist speaks of "yesterday" as being comparable to "a
thousand years" in the Lord's sight. It is, however, not *hindsight*
with which Second Peter is dealing but rather *foresight*. Consequently, he alters the Psalm to read, "with the Lord one day is as
a thousand years, and a thousand years as one day" (vs. 8). And
his argument assumes that Jesus' promise of his "coming" was of
the most general sort, in line with the prophetic teaching regarding "the day of the Lord," which began, so far as our information
leads us to believe, with Amos (see Amos 5:18). This "day,"
argues our author on the basis of Psalm 90:4, is not to be reckoned with any yardstick known to man. It is God's day and is to
be calculated only by such method of reckoning as he employs.

Consequently, it is fallacious to argue that, inasmuch as "the
fathers . . . [have fallen] asleep," the promise has failed. This could
only be true if Jesus in making the promise had stated it in terms
of man's chronological reckoning, *and our author assumes that
he never did any such thing.* Instead, we should assume that the
apparent "slowness" about the promise's fulfillment is due to the
fact that the Lord "is forbearing" and "not wishing that any
should perish, but that all should reach repentance" (vs. 9). We
should rather "count the forbearance of our Lord as salvation"
(vs. 15; compare Luke 13:8; Rom. 3:25-26; Heb. 12:5-8; I Peter
3:20; Rev. 6:9-11; 9:20-21).

The author now concludes his second argument, adding to his
own original formulation of it a thought which must have become
by his day a commonplace in Christian thinking—namely, that
"the day of the Lord will come like a thief" (vs. 10). According
to the Gospel writers, Jesus himself had taught this (see Matt.
24:43; Luke 12:39; and compare Mark 13:35-36); it was also

the teaching of the Apostle Paul (see I Thess. 5:2-6); and it is
found also in the Revelation to John (3:3; 16:15). The description
of the end which follows (vs. 10) is a repetition in slightly different terms of what we have already seen (vs. 7; see also vss.
11-13).

But the end of God's purpose for mankind is not destruction.
The author adds to his twofold reply to the scoffers the assurance,
which is common to the Scriptures first and last, that God is more
than Judge; he is also Savior and Re-creator. It is true that "the
heavens will be kindled and dissolved, and the elements will melt
with fire" (vs. 12). This is by no means all that "the coming of the
day of God" will mean for mankind, for "his promise" includes
the coming of "new heavens and a new earth in which righteousness dwells" (vs. 13). And it is because Christians look for this
re-creation that they realize that they should order their lives in
"holiness and godliness" (vs. 11).

This teaching with regard to "new heavens and a new earth"
goes back to Isaiah 65:17; 66:22. And it is a major theme in the
Revelation to John (see chs. 21 and 22) as of other apocalyptic
writings. The thought is fundamental to the prophetic conception
of the nature of God as a God of righteousness, grace, and truth.
Second Peter does not explain how Christians may further the
"hastening" of the "coming of the day of God" (vs. 12). But, in
the context of his thought, we may perhaps conclude that "lives
of holiness and godliness" are the instruments which God has
placed at man's disposal for furthering this end (vs. 11).

EXHORTATION TO RIGHTEOUS LIVING

II Peter 3:14-18

The author devotes the last section of his sermon and letter to
an exhortation to his Christian readers to live "lives of holiness
and godliness" (see vs. 11), or as he now says, "be zealous to be
found by him without spot or blemish, and at peace" (vs. 14).
This is to say that the Final Coming and the Judgment, together
with the thought of "new heavens and a new earth in which
righteousness dwells" (vs. 13), are to serve as the Christian's
motive for right living. The motive of fear, it should be observed,
is not suggested. Nor is there anything morbid about the motive
which he does suggest. The point is the one found everywhere

throughout the Scriptures of the Old and New Testaments: that God is both Judge and Savior of mankind, and that man is always to live his life in righteousness and peace, in love and truth, because God is a God of holiness and righteousness who demands that man shall so live his life (see I Peter 1:15-16). Man is not taught to live in terror of this holy God, but rather simply to "count the forbearance of our Lord as salvation" (vs. 15; see vs. 9 above). In closing, accordingly, the author returns to the first theme of the letter, suggesting that it is the function of Christians to "grow in the grace and knowledge of our Lord and Savior Jesus Christ" (vs. 18; see 1:2, 5-11). Such growth will lead to a deepening understanding of the nature of God and at the same time induce in us a like nature.

In the midst of his exhortation Second Peter again warns his readers against "the error of lawless men," that is, presumably, the scoffers of whom he has been speaking (vs. 17; see 2:17-22; 3:3-7). And again identifying himself with the Apostle Peter, he refers to the manner in which his "beloved brother Paul" wrote. He declares that there are "some things" in Paul's letters which are "hard to understand" (vs. 16)—presumably, in the present context, a doctrine like Paul's "glorious liberty of the children of God" (Rom. 8:21). Such a doctrine, says the author, "the ignorant and unstable twist to their own destruction" (converting liberty into licentiousness), and it is clear from Paul's own writing that this statement is in accordance with the facts (see his argument at Rom. 6:1-23).

Second Peter ends his letter with a benediction: "To him be the glory both now and to the day of eternity. Amen." The term "glory" stands alone as in Romans 16:27 and Hebrews 13:21, a phenomenon, however, which is in accordance with the general thought of Second Peter that man is to reflect the glory of God (see 1:3, 17). The expression "the day of eternity" is found nowhere else in the New Testament. It is clearly intended to refer to the total extent of the eternal order and no doubt is a reflection of the teaching in verses 8-9.